Program Evaluation and
Review Technique:

Applications in Education

Desmond L. Cook

University Press
of America™

Copyright © 1979 by

University Press of America, Inc.™

4710 Auth Place, S.E., Washington, D.C. 20023

Library of Congress Catalog Card Number: 78-57981

Foreword

FEDERAL SUPPORT for research in education has increased substantially during the past decade and has now become a multimillion dollar operation. Basic research, development, and demonstration projects ranging in size from less than a thousand to over a million dollars are being supported by the Office of Education. It is mandatory that each project be conducted as economically as possible; thus all projects need to be managed. While projects involving one or two persons can create few management problems, those projects which involve several persons and many activities will require management techniques for effective operation. There is no single way for effectively managing a large project, but the Program Evaluation and Review Technique (PERT), which is discussed in this monograph, should prove to be a beneficial tool for the practitioner.

The Department of Defense, for example, uses PERT in many of its research efforts, and it is hoped that persons who are interested in educational research will make similar use of this PERT management technique. This monograph discusses the characteristics of PERT and describes methods of applying or implementing PERT on research and development projects pertaining to education. The monograph should be especially useful to educational research administrators, project directors, and professors who teach research methodology and management.

GLENN C. BOERRIGTER
Research Coordinator,
Research Branch

A publication of the

BUREAU OF RESEARCH

R. Louis Bright, *Associate Commissioner*

Division of Elementary-Secondary Research
Richard Suchman, *Officer in Charge*

Research Branch
Howard F. Hjelm, *Director*

Preface

THE PURPOSE OF THIS MONOGRAPH is to disseminate to the educational community the basic concepts and principles of a recently developed project management information system entitled Program Evaluation and Review Technique—or PERT. It is anticipated that creating awareness of the technique's existence will lead to its adoption as a project planning and control tool for research and development activities. This monograph is not designed to be an exhaustive treatment, but its primary goal is to establish sufficient knowledge about the technique to enable individuals desiring to implement PERT to do so. A selected bibliography is presented for persons desiring further instruction.

The preparation of this monograph was made possible through a contract with the Cooperative Research Branch of the U.S. Office of Education which permitted me to study the technique. The specific activity funded was Project E–019, "The Applicability of PERT to Educational Research and Development Activities," which was carried out from March 1, 1964 to August 31, 1965.

I am indebted to many organizations, both military and civilian, for assistance in formulating the basic concepts and principles of PERT and wish to express special thanks for the continued interest and cooperation provided by the PERT Orientation and Training Center, Washington, D.C.

I am particularly indebted to Dr. Earl Stahl, Assistant Project Director, for his assistance in preparing the chapter on basic characteristics of PERT and for his help with the many activities involved in completing this project. A special acknowledgment is owed to Ian Seeds, Missile Program Control Manager, Columbus Division of the North American Aviation Company, for giving me the benefit of his extended experiences in PERT application, and for his critical and detailed review of the manuscript in its draft form. I wish to thank my colleagues at The Ohio State University for their assistance in helping with the study of the PERT technique by direct application to on-going projects. I would also like to extend my appreciation to Terry Owen,

Research Assistant, who became an expert on PERT computer programs, and to Mrs. Judy Eby, Project Secretary, for typing the final manuscript. To all of the above persons and agencies I am deeply grateful. The ultimate responsibility for accuracy and consistency is mine alone.

DESMOND L. COOK

Contents

Appendixes

Figures

Chapter 1

Management Process in Educational Research and Development

THE TWO DECADES since termination of World War II have witnessed increased emphasis on research and development activities in almost all areas of the economy. Research and development has always existed in an advancing technological society, but it was during the years of conflict that initiation of such broad, large-scale research projects as the Manhattan project, dealing with complex and often relatively new concepts and ideas, began to reach fruition. While industry has been concerned primarily with research and development relating to the development of new products and improvement of those existing, or the creating of new markets, the emphasis given to basic research has been much less impressive. The government, on the other hand, has utilized both basic and applied research and development for the design of new military weapon systems. More recently, government-industry partnership in conducting large-scale research and development activities has been stressed.

The advent of a new "look" in research and development activities has created many problems for project managers and personnel. In general, achievement of a stated goal depends upon how well the end objective has been specified, past experience in accomplishing such goals, and the application of resources. For example, successful completion of a vacation trip to a specified site is more likely to succeed because of prior experience with such an undertaking; however, in putting a man on the moon, a low initial probability exists because of relative inexperience even though the goal is well defined. Probability of success with either increases with the excellence of any "road map" used.

Numerous techniques and systems have been developed, and while they have been generally successful when applied to relatively small-scale projects where production is often routine, such management systems would be of limited usefulness for new large-scale and highly complex—both quantitatively and qualitatively—research and development projects.

In the specific case of new military weapons system, because of increasing difficulty in properly managing all activities associated with its development using traditional techniques, a search began for new methods of handling a multitude of unknown and complex tasks. In 1958, the Special Projects Office of the Navy Department developed a system designed to provide for more effective project control. The basic need for this system appeared when the Navy Department and the prime contractors determined that their project had many dissimilar operations, widely dispersed geographically. Different contractor management systems had to be correlated, resulting in the Program Evaluation and Review Technique management system, to which the acronym PERT has been applied. Since numerous historical accounts of the development of PERT exist, the subject will not be repeated here. Background information appears in summary reports prepared by the Special Projects Office of the U.S. Navy (24, 25) and in an article by Malcolm and others (14)*. PERT is a methodology for *planning* many diverse activities regardless of their nature, and will be useful in either small or large projects. Because of its reported successful application to widely diverse activities (e.g., house construction, missile development, Broadway plays), its potential usefulness to the management of educational research and development activities has been recognized.

This monograph is designed to present to the educational research and development community the basic principles of PERT as well as suggestions for utilizing them in the management of educational research and development projects. These matters appear not to have caused great concern until given impetus by government and private support for research which increased tremendously during the past decade. Also, introduction of federal programs such as the Cooperative Research Program of 1954 and the National Defense Education Act of 1958 provided funds for a wide variety of research and development programs, and numerous private philanthropic organizations such as The Ford Foundation gave substantial monetary support. Large appropriations are being made for research and development activities under the new vocational education legislation passed by Congress in 1963 and the Elementary and Secondary Education Act of 1965.

Problems of government-industry research and development managers are now being faced by persons occupying parallel positions in education. Consequently, solutions developed by the former might be applicable to educational research and development management problems.

To facilitate understanding of the purpose and nature of a management information system such as PERT, the remainder of this chapter

---

* Numbers in parentheses refer to the bibliographic listing in the Appendix to this report.

will be devoted to a brief discussion of a definition of management, a description of the management process, and the characteristics of a good management system, concluding with a rationale for applying management concepts to educational research and development projects and programs.

The Nature of Management

Management is defined here as the art and science of planning, organizing, motivating, and controlling human and material resources and their interaction in order to attain a predetermined objective. As viewed here, management is a broader activity than is administration. The former focuses on a process of decision-making which is considered to be one of the tasks of management, while the latter focuses on implementation of policy and the provision of administrative support to research programs. The director of an educational research and development project is basically a manager. He alone is responsible for all decisions about the use of people and resources. One or more offices on a campus (including computer centers, publications offices, and travel bureaus), can assist with administrative matters, but they cannot direct decision-making.

The term *management* in educational circles has not had wide acceptance, yet the activities that educational personnel often perform are more appropriately managerial than administrative. This fact has been well pointed out by Hungate (9). Presidents and deans are managers to the degree that they plan the course of future events and activities, organize, motivate people to carry out plans, assess progress, and control the results. Under this concept, managers have line responsibilities while administrators have staff responsibilities.

The Management Process

The process involved in moving from initiating a project or program to the final objective consists of several broad procedural steps (12). While some variation may result from uniqueness of an individual project, the general activities involved in management are illustrated in figure 1.

Planning.—Before any project is initiated, the major and subordinate objectives must be identified in order to accomplish the overall objective. In addition, project objectives must be presented to staff members. Project objectives may consist of equipment, decisions, facilities, data, or services.

Figure 1.—The Management Cycle

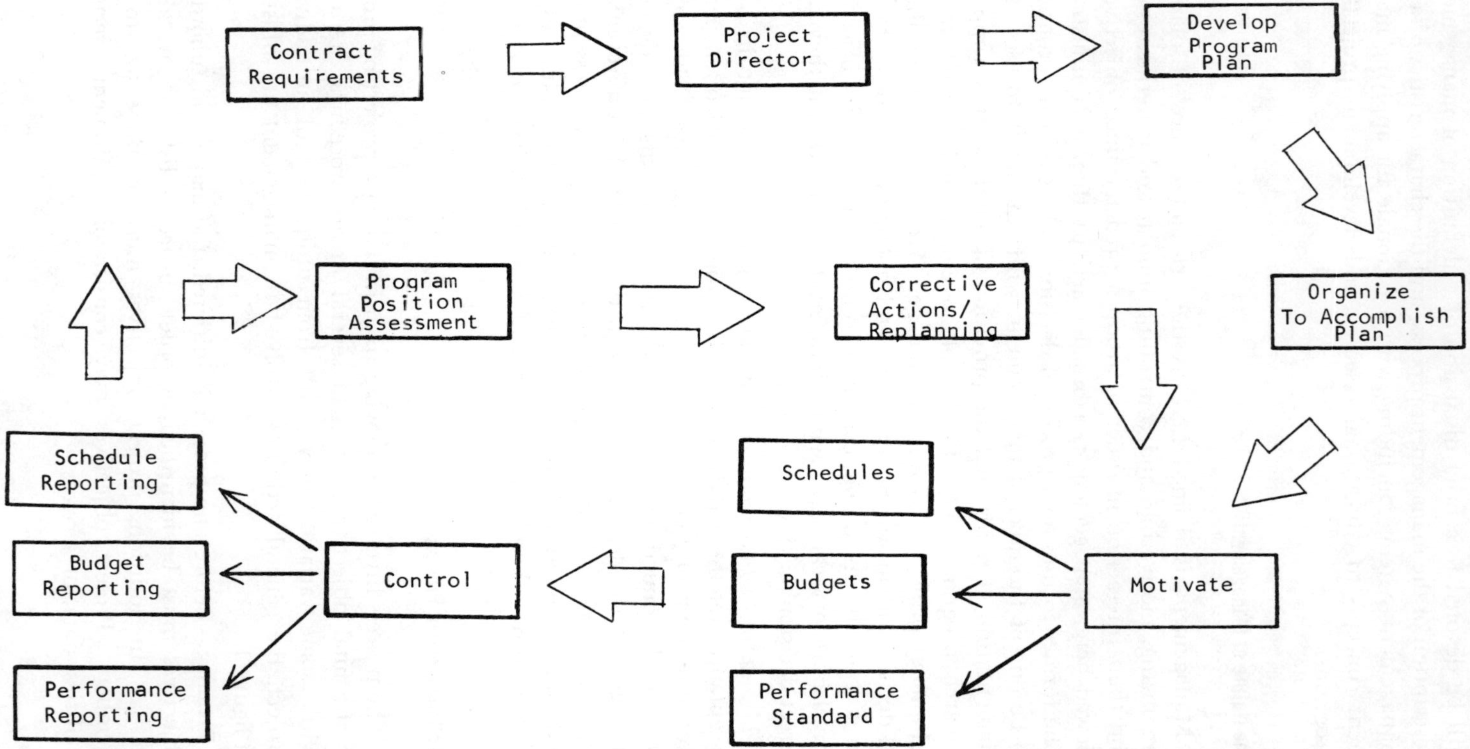

4

A general process for determining objectives is to proceed by a "top-down" approach, asking just what end items, operational systems, or services the project is to produce, and each of these will be further subdivided by ascertaining what facilities or services will be needed to complete each objective. Successive subdivisions, when required, will complete objectives above them. The process of program definition through subdivision and classification may reveal a need for establishment of additional higher level end items. The net result will insure that various program elements are properly identified and categorized. The manager must identify and organize program objectives, and then plan and employ resources to accomplish them. The top-down planning approach is used because it insures that program objectives are supported by lower-level objectives, that the overall project is integrated and parts interrelated, and that a useful way is provided to summarize program information.

Organizing.—Successful accomplishment of a total project depends fundamentally upon the establishment of a plan designed to reach major and minor objectives. Accomplishment of a program goal can be reached by any one of several possible plans, with broad latitude for flexibility in planning. Planning is interpreted here to include not only a careful definition of program end objectives but also the effort involved in determining specific work or tasks and establishing the sequence and dependency existing among the tasks, along with performance standards or quality control levels. The goal is to achieve an optimum balance between schedule, costs, and performance requirements.

Once the plan has been established, calendar dates and times can be ascertained for start and completion of each element of the plan within allowable time periods; this process is referred to as *scheduling*. Once duration times have been allocated, manpower requirements can be determined. Scheduling is considered to be fundamentally different from planning in that the latter considers the logic or sequence of activities while scheduling specifies beginning and cutoff dates for each segment of the program plan.

Motivating.—After planning and organizing are accomplished, the motivation of personnel will be of primary importance. This management step will include communicating project goals, directing assignment of tasks between departments and/or persons providing competent leadership, assessing staff morale, and similar actions. Good management involves communication between all levels of management, from the main project supervisor down to the line supervisor. Involvement of all concerned departments and personnel in planning and organizing functions will bring rewards in terms of increased morale and better production.

Controlling.—Once the project is underway, management must be kept fully informed of the status of the work on a regular basis and upon request; deviations must be called to the attention of management along with recommendations for corrective action. Controlling is the process of action by management in response to deviations from the schedule.

One major problem in project control is to know or to identify those project elements or tasks which require management attention. Not all problems are of equal intensity. Proper project control involves utilization of the "management by exception" principle under which the best use is made of management competencies by directing them to crucial problems and not to minor or less crucial matters properly handled by subordinates.

After reaching a solution to a problem, the manager may have to modify or incorporate new elements or revise old elements of the plan. The general success of such a replanning effort will be noted by the degree to which the new plan can be carried out in subsequent time.

Integrated Management System

Any system or technique designed to aid management must facilitate manipulation of three common dimensions of a project— (a) *time,* (b) *cost* (or resources) , and (c) *performance.*

The *time* dimension consists basically of those aspects of a project relating to the time that each work element is expected to consume plus the total time for finalization of the project. Time overruns on individual activities can delay the end completion date. Time underruns, on the other hand, while leading to early completion, might reflect inefficient application of program resources and/or inadequate program definition.

The *cost* dimension involves allocation of resources (men, materials, equipment, and money). Consumption of materials and manpower at a rate faster than planned might result in a cost overrun or overexpenditure of budget for the total project. On the other hand, a decision to spend faster in order to achieve an early completion target may have no adverse effects on the project.

The *performance* dimension refers essentially to levels of quality stated as end objective specifications. For example, developmental specifications for a school test might require that it have a test-retest coefficient of .90 based upon a 1 percent national sample of high school seniors.

Generally, the project manager must manipulate time and cost dimensions in order to accomplish the specified technical performance level. Successful attainment of performance levels may require additional time and money, resulting in overruns. Rigid limitations on the time-cost dimensions, such as exist in fixed-price contracts, may result in a decision to lower performance specifications.

A total and integrated management system must provide useful and timely information to the appropriate management level. This information must compare actual with planned status in the areas of schedule, cost, and performance. In addition, good analysis of problem situations by the staff can greatly increase the effectiveness of line management.

Applying Management Concepts to Education

Why should the educational community be interested in the application of management concepts to research and development? In addition to the lack of experience previously cited, other answers are discussed below without regard to relative importance.

Research and development projects possess certain common characteristics regardless of their individual nature. Each research and development project has a starting and end point, with the latter usually being carefully delineated. To reach an end objective, a series of tasks must be accomplished in some prescribed order. Since many persons and/or organizations are involved, some type of coordinate effort must be arranged. Furthermore, much uncertainty will exist with regard to the nature of tasks to be performed and the time available. Such projects are sometimes referred to as "once-through" activities since the project may not be repeated unless it develops into a routine and production-type undertaking. Also lacking will be guidelines such as full historical and background information and standards for determining time, sequences, and methods of reaching goals.

Military and industrial projects evidence the above characteristics, as well as many educational research and development activities. Many kinds of activities such as curriculum development, test construction, or making a school survey, may have these characteristics. A system or technique which might help to overcome problems associated with research and development would be useful to administrators and other personnel involved.

Perhaps a more cogent reason than project characteristics for examining management concepts centers around the evolutionary, and perhaps even revolutionary, change taking place with regard to funding of the educational research and development effort. During the past decade, the amount of research support available for educational activities has grown tremendously. Hungate (9) noted that $30 million were available from various sources in 1954, $50 million in 1958, and almost $1 billion in 1963. Recent legislation by Congress has further increased funds.

While an increase in research support usually is accepted as being desirable, certain restrictions are an inherent part of securing these funds. Agencies allocating money usually require some type of project proposal along with a budget statement and progress reports at selected intervals. By various means, projects are monitored from the beginning or initial funding to achievement of the objective, which often includes submission of a final technical report.

Extensive funding of research and development has resulted in a change in the nature of projects in that they are becoming much larger and more complex in scope, and often involve a research team as opposed to a single researcher. Not uncommonly, government-funded educational research and development projects are from 3 to 5 years in duration, involve a staff of 10 to 15 persons, and cost in excess of $500,000. The project director in this situation becomes a manager as well as a researcher. Whatever his personal desires might be, he must spend increasing amounts of time in the management process. Some aspects of his responsibilities are assumed by campus agencies such as research foundations, but in the long run, they serve primarily as facilitative agencies which can contribute significantly to the effectiveness of a researcher. A system which would assist managers of large as well as small projects in determining and controlling time and costs might allow more time for research and lessen time devoted to management.

As noted above, one feature of the increased support for educational research is the requirement for a research proposal to be prepared, usually in accordance with a format supplied by the funding agency, and to include the purpose of this research, general procedures to be followed, a statement of needed staffing, and a proposed division of costs. The proposal usually satisfies these requirements, but when a project is underway, many difficulties may occur because of inadequate planning in the proposal stage. Interdependencies between project objectives are not adequately clarified, nor are key milestone progression points clearly identified. Personnel requirements are often established without realistically relating activities to skills and/or time requirements. Since good management is facilitated by good planning, knowledge of a system designed to improve such planning would result in better management and would increase the probability of successful completion of objectives.

*   *   *

The purpose of this monograph is to present such a technique developed for one aspect of research and development—project management. Specifically, attention will be given to the presentation of a management information system known as Program Evaluation and Review Technique, or PERT. The technique has been found to be significantly useful in the internal management of projects, the reporting of progress on a consistent basis to the funding agency, and as a tool to be used by that agency in evaluating the proposed plan for research. In view of PERT's success in effective program management in many areas of government funding, it is not unreasonable to assume that such a system would be required as part of educational research and development projects or programs. Expenditures within the jurisdiction of the Department of Defense include PERT or other formalized management systems as an integral part of the procurement cycle.

Chapter II

Basic Characteristics of PERT

THIS CHAPTER IS designed to present the general features of PERT in order to acquaint potential users with basic concepts, techniques, and methods of the system. Application of these features will vary with the situation, depending upon complexity of the project involved and reasons for adoption of the PERT system.

Topics covered in this chapter are: work breakdown structure; network development; activity time estimation; network time calculations; scheduling; probability aspects of PERT; replanning the project; and an introduction to PERT/COST.

Work Breakdown Structure

The use of PERT as a technique for project management begins with a definition of project objectives. The Work Breakdown Structure, which reflects a top-down approach to planning, should serve as the initial step in applying PERT. This process consists of subdividing a total project into smaller and more easily managed elements. The process of subdivision and classification continues until the desired level of detail is reached.

A Work Breakdown Structure for a simple survey project is shown as figure 2. The major units of work are objectives, design, data analysis, and documentation, identified as Level (1).

Figure 2.—Major Work Units of a Simple Survey Project

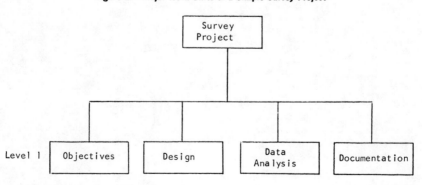

10

Figure 3 illustrates a further subdivision of the design, along with a classification of work at the next lower level for the design subdivision labeled as Sample.

A further breakdown would identify the components of each unit, as shown in figure 3. Thereafter, dependency relationships existing between components would be depicted by use of a network.

A Work Breakdown Structure may also be developed using the format illustrated in figure 4, showing four major work units under Level (1), the components of each unit under Level (2), and the work packages under Level (3). Some components are not broken down at the third level because they are considered to be small enough for planning and control at Level (2).

Network Development

A *network* is the foundation of the **PERT** system. It shows the plan established to reach project objectives, interrelationship and interdependencies of project elements, and priorities of the elements of the plan. In essence, the network is a graphic representation of the project plan.

Determination of the networking system is ascertained by the project work breakdown structure which must be constructed as an initial step in project planning. For relatively simple projects, the use of a single network may suffice. In complex programs, a master network will be developed depicting the total program. The complexity of the work breakdown structure will then provide the basis for establishing the number and type of subnetworks. For example, subnetworks may be constructed for each one of the first-level program elements, or if the project is sufficiently complex, for each of lower level elements. Each subnetwork is an expansion of the detail in a particular of the master network.

A network is composed of *events* and *activities*. *Events* represent the start or completion of an activity and do not consume time, personnel, or resources. Events are instantaneous points in time when an action has been started or completed.

The following are examples of event descriptions:

Start sample selection.
Start test item analysis.
Start writing curriculum guide.
Complete statistical analysis.
Complete enrollment survey.
Complete literature review.

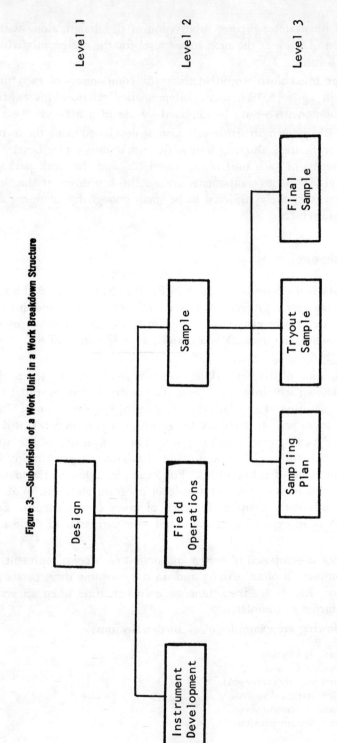

Figure 3.—Subdivision of a Work Unit in a Work Breakdown Structure

Level 1

Level 2

Level 3

Design

Instrument
Development

Field
Operations

Sample

Sampling
Plan

Tryout
Sample

Final
Sample

Figure 4.—Work Breakdown Structure for a Simple Survey Project

	LEVEL 1	LEVEL 2	LEVEL 3
Survey Project	Objectives	Problem Delimitation Hypotheses Data Paradigms	
	Survey Design	Instrument Development	Item Construction Format Design Direction Preparation Cover Letter Preparation Tryout Item Revision Final Form Production
		Field Operations	Travel Arrangements Interviewer Selection Reliability Check Follow-up Procedures
		Sample	Sampling Plan Tryout Sample Final Sample
	Data Analysis	Coding System Data Reduction Statistical Tests Interpretation	
	Documentation	Narrative Tables/Graphs Bibliography	

The general practice is to represent events in a network by the use of circles. Squares, rectangles, and other symbols are sometimes used to designate project milestones or most important events.

In the event that more than one network is developed for a project, the use of *interface events* will be necessary. An interface event is an event signaling a necessary transfer of responsibility, information, or end items, from one part of a plan to another. These events tie the subnetworks and master networks together in a single structure for purposes of total program planning and control.

13

An *activity* is a task or job in the project requiring utilization of personnel and resources over a period of time. An activity consists of the work processes leading from one event to another. Activity descriptions must be as definitive as possible in order that work responsibilities can be assigned, realistic time estimates can be made throughout duration of the activity, and users of the network may understand the purpose of each activity in the whole scheme.

The following are examples of activity descriptions:

> Select statistical technique.
> Keypunch data cards.
> Write questionnaire items.
> Hire new staff.
> Install audiovisual equipment.
> Design test manual.

An activity is represented on the network by an arrow connecting one event with another. Dummy activities—those which do not consume time or resources—are represented by dotted arrows. An example of a simplified network is shown in figure 5.

The construction of a network requires that certain rules be observed in order to insure clear and precise logic. A network may have to be reviewed several times to avoid violations.

The first step in constructing a network is to place project work units, as identified in the Work Breakdown Structure, in their logical order. Supporting events and activities may then be added to form the network.

Figure 5.—Simplified Network Showing Events, Activities, and Dummy Activities

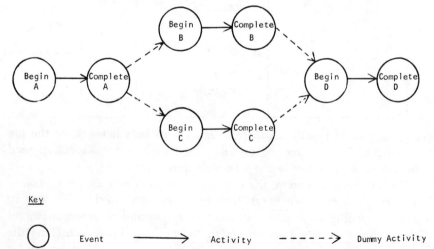

The question of whether a network is constructed from the beginning to the end event (left to right or forward), or from the end to the beginning event (right to left or backward), somewhat depends upon the uniqueness of the project. If elements of the project are fairly well known and defined, a forward-type construction might be employed. On the other hand, a backward construction forces the user to consider what activities and events must take place before project objectives can be accomplished. Whichever method is used, the flow of the network always moves from left to right.

Dependency and *constraint* are fundamental concepts of network construction. A dependency or *real* constraint exists when one activity or event cannot take place until the events and activities preceding it have been completed. *Planned* constraints, however, are those event/activity relationships which have been established as a desirable but not absolutely necessary program relationship. Various types of dependency and constraint situations are illustrated below: [1]

1. **Series Construction.**—A series (or linear) construction is used when the dependencies form a progressive or additive chain as illustrated in figure 6.

Figure 6.—Series Construction

2. **Parallel Construction.**—A parallel construction is used when two or more concurrent activities are constraining a common subsequent event. Note that in figure 7, any activity following event 4 cannot begin until activities 2–4 and 3–4 are complete.

Figure 7.—Parallel Construction

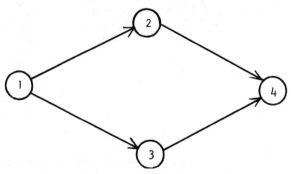

---

[1] The illustrations and accompanying explanations are reproduced by permission of General Precision, Inc., Commercial Computer Division, 100 East Tujunga Avenue, Burbank, Calif.

15

3. **Burst Construction.**—In a burst construction, illustrated in figure 8, several succeeding events are constrained by a single predecessor event. If no time is consumed between the single predecessor event and the dependent events, dummy activities are used.

Figure 8.—Burst Construction

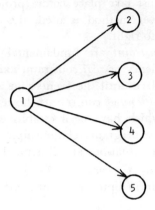

4. **Merge Construction.**—The merge construction in figure 9 illustrates a single successor event being dependent upon the completion of several preceding activities. Dummy activities may also be used if no time is involved.

Figure 9.—Merge Construction

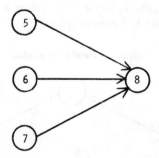

5. **Network Clarity.**—The clarity and accuracy of a network depends upon the illustration of start and completion of each activity included. This is done through the use of "start" events, "complete" events, and dummy activities. If an activity cannot start before a preceding activity is finished, only start or complete events need be indicated as shown in figure 10.

Figure 10.—Designation of Start and Completion of Activities for Network Clarity

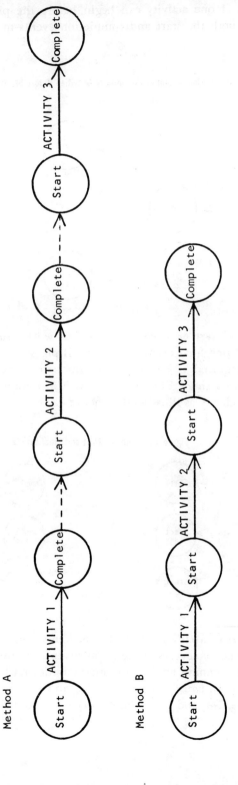

17

However, if one activity can begin before the preceding activity is completed, both the start and completion events must be shown as in figure 11.

Figure 11.—Required Completion of Preliminary Activities Before Starting Subsequent Activities

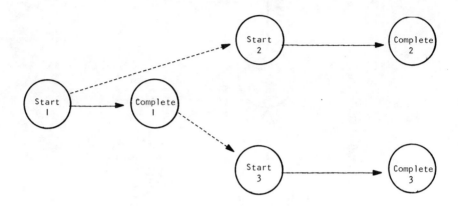

6. **Multiple Start or Final Events.**—A network usually has only one starting and one final event. While multiple start and end events are sometimes required, it is general procedure to tie multiple start and/or end events to a single dummy event with a dummy activity arrow for purposes of clarity as illustrated in figure 12.

Figure 12.—Dummy Start and Final Events

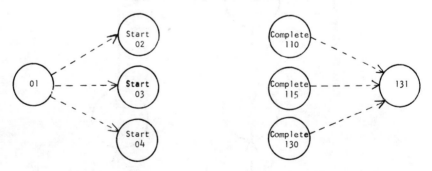

7. **Concurrent Activity Construction.**—Only one activity may be shown between two events. Where concurrent activities are being carried out between common events, dummy activities must be used to set off the activities. In figure 13, activities 1–2 and 1–3 are dummies allowing activities 1–4, 2–4, and 3–4 to be illustrated as occurring concurrently.

18

Figure 13.—Concurrent Activity Construction

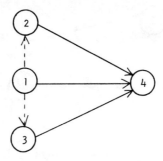

8. **Concurrent Activities With Different Dependencies.**—Dummy activities are used to clarify dependencies where concurrent activities are not dependent upon a single preceding activity or event. In the example below (figure 14), activity 3–5 is dependent upon the completion of activities 1–3 and 2–4. Activity 4–6 is only dependent upon the completion of activity 2–4.

Figure 14.—Concurrent Activities With Different Dependencies

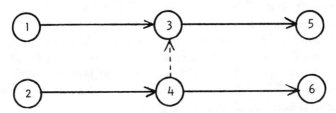

In addition to the network construction techniques illustrated, some further rules imposed on networking are listed below:

1. An event is unique and can occur only once in a network.
2. There can be no feedbacks or loops in the network. That is, the network cannot return to an event that has been accomplished.

A general procedure in the PERT technique is to identify the network paths by the events through which they pass. Figure 15 illustrates a network with three paths; i.e., 1–2–6, 1–4–·6, and 1–3–5–6.

Activity Time Estimation

After the network has been constructed and its logic approved by users, the estimated time to complete each step is secured. A single time estimate may be secured for the expected duration of an activity, but the more usual procedure is to secure three time estimates in cases where

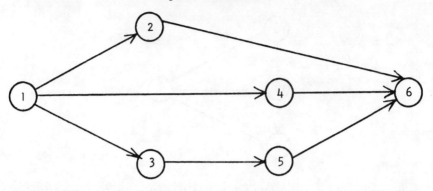

Figure 15.—Network Paths

uncertainty regarding work scope must be considered. These three estimates are known as the *Most Likely Time,* the *Optimistic Time,* and the *Pessimistic Time.*

The *Most Likely Time* is that which, in the estimator's judgment, the activity will consume under normal circumstances. The *Optimistic Time* is the least amount of time the activity will take under the most optimum conditions. This estimate assumes that work involved in an activity will progress with exceptional ease and speed, but, would have no more than one chance in a hundred of being completed in this time. The *Pessimistic Time* assumes that anything that can will go wrong, short of acts of God. This estimate should take into account the most adverse conditions including the possibility of failures occurring which require new starts. This time estimate also has no more than one chance in a hundred of occurring.

The basic statistical assumption of PERT is that the three time estimates form a Beta distribution, and experience has substantiated this appraisal. Figure 16 presents an example of a Beta curve with an Optimistic (*a*) and Pessimistic (*b*) time forming the range of the distribution and the Most Likely Time (*m*) appearing at the mode of the curve.

No standard procedure exists regarding the order in which the three time estimates must be secured. Most users of PERT, however, estimate the Most Likely Time followed by the Optimistic and Pessimistic Times.

It is important that activity duration times be secured from the person responsible for accomplishment of an activity. Those imposed by uninformed management or higher authority are not consistent with the PERT system. It is also important that the individual activities on a network be estimated in a random manner to avoid biasing the time estimate of an activity by an estimate given for an activity immediately preceding or succeeding it.

20

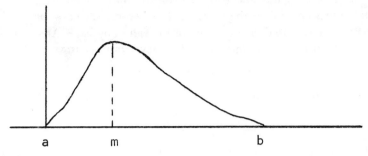

Figure 16.—Beta Distribution of the Three Time Estimates

a   m   b

The validity of time estimates will depend to a large degree on how well the activity is defined. Since the validity of output data from the PERT system depends directly on the validity of time estimates, activity definition becomes quite important. Vague or gross activity definitions are difficult to time precisely.

The uniqueness or newness of work involved also will affect time estimates for an activity; if operations have been performed many times before, these estimates may have a very small range, such as 4–5–6. It is even possible that values of the three estimates may be the same if the nature and duration of an activity are well established. On the other hand, unique and seldom performed activities will be characteristized by time estimates with wide ranges, such as 2–6–12. This uniqueness of tasks and activities is inherent in many research and development efforts, and the three time estimates are intended to allow for this uncertainty. Other conditions usually prevailing are:

1. Time estimates assume that resources (including personnel) will be available on a normal basis or as requested in the project proposal.

2. Time estimates are based on a 5-day work week and are established by weeks and tenths of weeks. A time estimate of 0.1 week would be equivalent to ½ of a day; an estimate of 0.2 would be equivalent to 1 day; and so forth. Other time units may be used, but the week and tenth of a week are most common.

3. Schedule or calendar dates should have no effect on initial time estimates. By ignoring present calendar dates, the estimator avoids biasing his estimates in favor of these dates.

Network Time Calculations

After the three time estimates have been secured, average or *Expected Elapsed times* are calculated for each activity using the following formula:

$$t_e = \frac{a + 4m + b}{6}$$

21

In this formula, t_e is the Expected Elapsed time, a the Optimistic time, m the Most Likely time, and b the Pessimistic time.

Total values entered in the formula thus become six $(a + 4m + 1b)$, making it necessary to divide the sum of the values by six. [2] An example of using the three time estimates in the above formula is:

$$a = 5$$
$$m = 10$$
$$b = 14$$
$$t_e = \frac{5 + (4)\ (10) + 14}{6}$$
$$t_e = \frac{59}{6}$$
$$t_e = 9.8$$

The calculated t_e values are customarily rounded off to the nearest tenth of a week.

After the Expected Elapsed time has been computed for an activity, one can also obtain an estimate of the variability of time estimates associated with it. The range of time spread is represented by the standard deviation of the activity times. The formula for finding the standard deviation is:

$$\sigma_{t_e} = \frac{b - a}{6}$$

substituting the values used in the above example,

$$b = 14,\ a = 5$$
$$\sigma_{t_e} = \frac{14 - 5}{6}$$
$$\sigma_{t_e} = 1.5$$

The obtained value can be used to estimate the probability that an activity will be completed within the range of estimated times by employing normal curve concepts. For an example, a 68 percent chance exists that the activity will be completed within 1.5 weeks either side of the Expected Elapsed time (t_e), a 95 percent chance that the activity will be completed within 3 weeks either side of t_e, and a 99 percent chance that the activity will be completed within 4.5 weeks of t_e. An additional explanation of the statistical assumptions is presented in several references listed in the Annotated Bibliography in the appendix section of this report.

---

[2] A discussion of the origin and validity of the formulas for the mean and variance based upon the assumed Beta distribution appears in MacCrimmon and Ryavec (13) and hence, such considerations are not presented in this monograph.

The Expected Elapsed time (t_e) provides a means for determining the earliest and latest times in which any given event can take place. The earliest time is designated as the *Earliest Expected Time* and is represented by the symbol T_E, while the latest time is designated as *Latest Allowable Time* and is represented by the symbol T_L.

Figure 17 presents an example of computing T_E for network events. Since no activities or events precede Event 1, the T_E at Event 1 is 0. To find the T_E for any subsequent event, the t_e's are summed along the *longest* path to the given event. For example, the t_e for Activity 1–2 is 2, therefore, the T_E for Event 2 is 2. At Event 5, there are two possible T_E's since two activity paths merge at this event. The rule for selecting the T_E for an event where two or more activity paths merge is to select the one that yields the largest value. In the example, activity path 1–2–5 has a total t_e value of 5.6 while path 1–3–4–5 has a total t_e value of 10. Therefore, the T_E at Event 5 is 10 weeks.

Figure 17.—Computing T_E's for Network Events

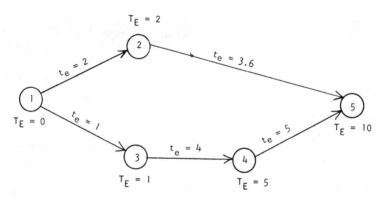

The Latest Allowable Time (T_L) for each event is computed by beginning with the final or end event and subtracting the t_e's of preceding activities. The T_L is the latest time by which an event must occur without causing a delay in accomplishment of the final event. For purposes of illustration, the value of 10 weeks was assigned as the T_L value at Event 5. The T_E value for Event 5 is 10 as derived in figure 17. Subtracting activity t_e's from T_L of 10 weeks results in T_L values of 5 at Event 4 (10 — 5), 1 at Event 3 (5 — 4), and 6.4 at Event 2 (10 — 3.6). When two pathways merge at a single event, the smallest value for the two paths merging is selected as the T_L for that event. In figure 18, pathway 5–2–1 yields a T_L value of 4.4 for Event 1 while pathway 5–4–3–1 yields a T_L value of 0. The latter value is assigned as the T_L for Event 1.

Having found the T_E and T_L for each event, the amount of *slack* associated with these events can be computed. Slack for each event can

23

be determined by subtracting the T_E from the T_L. Figure 19 presents the computation of slack using the T_E and T_L values illustrated in figures 17 and 18.

Figure 18.—Computing T_L's for Network Events

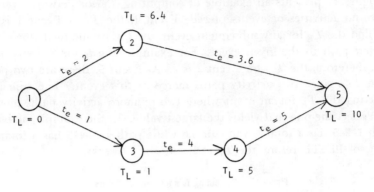

In many project situations, the amount of time available for completion of a project is either less or more than that estimated to accomplish the project in a desired manner, as represented by the T_E for the final event. When available time is less than estimated time, negative slack will exist along some or all network paths. This situation arises when the T_L value is smaller than the T_E value for all events along the negative slack path. Figure 20 presents a negative slack condition using the network in figure 19 with an available time of only

Figure 19.—Computing Slack

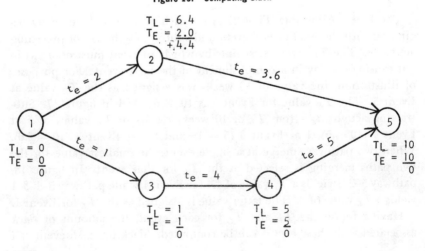

24

8, instead of 10 weeks. Events previously having 0 slack now have a negative 2 weeks of slack, while the slack associated with other events is reduced accordingly.

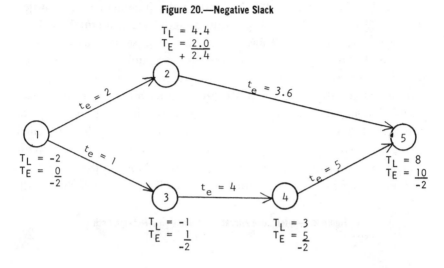

Figure 20.—Negative Slack

The slack condition arising when time available is greater than estimated time is referred to as positive slack. Using the same illustration as before, but now assuming an available time of 15 weeks instead of 10, figure 21 will show that large amounts of positive slack exist along the two pathways.

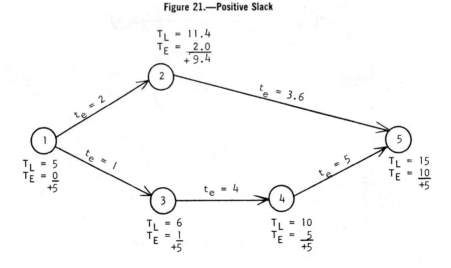

Figure 21.—Positive Slack

As noted in the discussion of figure 19, the amount of slack for events on path 1–3–4–5 is 0. Therefore, the activities on this path must be completed within their t_e values if Event 5 is to take place 10 weeks after Event 1: Path 1–2–5, however, has 4.4 weeks of slack. The distribution of this slack on path 1–2–5 is left to the judgment of the project director. For example, the beginning of activity 1–2 might be delayed 4.4 weeks after activity 1–3 has started. In this case, the slack has been eliminated. On the other hand, activities 1–2 and 2–5 could be completed in 5.6 weeks, at which time the resource application could be terminated, resulting automatically in elimination of slack along that path. These two alternatives are graphically displayed in figure 22. When slack has been allocated by either alternative, appropriate scheduled dates are assigned to beginning and terminating events in the path.

Slack in the network also identifies the *Critical Path* since it is defined as that path from the beginning to the ending event which has the

Figure 22.—Alternative Allocation of Slack on a Network Path

Alternative A

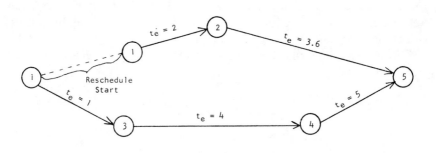

Alternative B

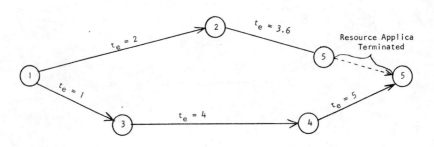

26

least amount of positive or the greatest amount of negative slack. It may also be defined as the longest or most time-consuming path through the network. The Critical Path is graphically displayed on the network by a double or heavier line as illustrated in figure 23.

Figure 23.—Critical Path

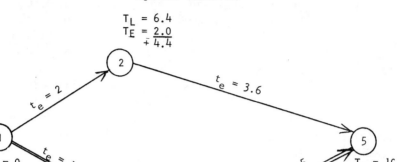

Activities on the Critical Path in the network provide the most rigid time constraint on completion of a project. The project director must focus his attention primarily on this path rather than upon those less critical. This feature of PERT provides a means of identifying critical areas or paths of the project which might go unrecognized until too late to prevent serious time slippages and costly overruns.

As the project progresses and the network is updated to reflect progress and changes in the plan, the Critical Path will often change in terms of activities and events through which it passes. Periodic updating of the network assures that the time significance of project changes will not go unnoticed.

Scheduling

The initial planning and time estimating for network activities purposely ignores calendar dates in order to avoid biasing time estimates in their favor. While the time estimates provide a framework for beginning the scheduling process, they do not supply all information needed.

The scheduling process is initiated by assigning a scheduled date (T_S) to significant events in the network. A scheduled date assigned to the end event must be the same as or earlier than the required project completion date. For example, a higher authority asks that the project be completed in 8 weeks. The project director, however, can assign a completion date of 6 weeks in order to offset unforeseen delays. In PERT terminology, a date imposed by an authority from outside the project is called a *Directed Date* (T_D) in order to distinguish it from a *Scheduled Date* established by the project director. A Scheduled Date for the final event in a network becomes the T_L for the end event, and is used to determine the T_L's for all other events.

Further scheduling is done by assigning Schedule Times (t_s) to activities in the network which may be the same, less, or greater than the expected time (t_e). The value of the t_s is dependent largely upon the project director's experience and knowledge concerning the activity. A scheduled earliest expected date (S_E) and a scheduled latest allowable date (S_L) may be computed for the network events in the same manner as for the event T_E's and T_L's, using the t_s values. Project schedules should be disseminated to personnel at the earliest possible time.

Several considerations are involved in scheduling a project, one being the real constraint imposed by availability of personnel, equipment, facilities, and other resources. For example, the use of elementary or high school students as subjects in a project usually is restricted to the months between September and June.

Another consideration involved is the desire for optimum utilization of personnel in order to avoid overtime or wasted hours. For example, project management could attempt to level manpower requirements by taking advantage of network slack, thus avoiding severely fluctuating manpower requirements. This is important because services of specialized personnel in an educational research and development project are often costly. If the nature of a project is such that these specialized services could be spread over the life of a project, or a large part of the project, rather than being peaked at some mid point, the project director might be able to devise a more realistic budget and a more realistic utilization of personnel. In some cases, the nature of a project could require specialized personnel and/or intermittent help, creating necessary high and low periods of manpower application. The utilization of PERT enables a project director to schedule well in advance all peak period personnel requirements.

Limitations of time and budget imposed by a funding agency also will affect scheduling of the project. For example, a project proposal may request a January 1 starting date. If the funding agency imposes a different date, such as April 1, the project director must internally schedule his project to meet this external requirement. Additionally, the funding agency or "customer" may impose other requirements that will affect the project schedule. For example, in a proposal to organize a foreign language curriculum for grades 1 through 4, the funding agency might ask to have grades 5 and 6 included. Such a request probably would add time and money to the original project plan and require modification of the schedule.

Finally there is the judgment of the project director as to reasonable time allotments for the various activities. If he knows that certain persons or departments tend to make pessimistic time estimates, he may impose schedule requirements inconsistent with the estimates based on past experience and judgment.

Probability Aspects of PERT

One feature of PERT which distinguishes it from other management systems is the use of probability theory as a predictive tool in forecasting the probable outcome of specific plans. The theory is applied in this manner:

Determine first the variance (σ^2) associated with each activity, using the following formula:

$$\sigma^2 = \left(\frac{b - a}{6} \right)^2$$

where b is the Pessimistic time estimate and a is the Optimistic time estimate.

Next find the standard deviation for any event in the network by summing activity variances on the longest path (in terms of time) through the network to the event in question and extracting the square root of this sum. The formula for finding event standard deviation is:

$$\sigma_{T_e} = \sqrt{\Sigma \sigma^2_{t_e}}$$

A statement of the probability of meeting any date is derived by using the standardized random variable "z" and normal probability tables. The formula is:

$$z = \frac{T_S - T_E}{\sigma_{T_E}}$$

where T_S equals the scheduled date, T_E equals the Earliest Expected Date, and σ_{T_E} is the standard deviation for the event in question.

Figure 24 illustrates the determination of probability of meeting a scheduled date for the end event in a network, it being Event 5 in this example. Beneath this network is the following information, listed from left to right: Activity; Optimistic time (a); Pessimistic time (b); Activity standard deviation (S.D.); Variance; Event No.; and Event standard deviation (S.D.). The scheduled date for Event 5 is 12 weeks while the T_E for this same event is 10 weeks.

Figure 24.—Determining the Probability of Meeting a Scheduled Date

Activity	a	b	S.D.	Variance	Event	Event S.D.
1 - 3	0.6	1.4	0.13	0.018	3	.018
3 - 4	4.0	4.0	0.00	0.000	4	.018
4 - 5	2.0	12.0	1.67	2.778	5	2.796
1 - 2	1.0	3.0	0.33	0.111	2	.111
2 - 5	2.8	4.6	0.30	0.090	5	.201

$$z = \frac{12 - 10}{1.672} = 1.196 = .85 \text{ Probability}$$

The z value of 1.196 has a probability of .85 in a normal curve table. Thus, the probability of completing Event 5 on time has been determined as 87 percent.

Although no firm ground rules have been established for interpreting probability data, 50 percent probability for event completion on schedule is considered ideal. Events with a probability of 84 percent or higher are considered undesirable as are those having less than a 15 percent probability of occurrence. Some PERT analysts view the 15 and 84 percent points as permitting too broad a band of deviation and, therefore, recommend 25 and 75 percent as "cut-off" points for low and high probability.

Replanning the Project

It is not uncommon in the first "run-through" of a network to obtain undesirable probability and slack conditions, usually resulting from a wish to establish an "ideal" project plan. When the ideal is not practical in terms of funding limitation, certain established generalized procedures can be applied for replanning networks, as follows:

1. *Removal of Planned Constraints.*—Planned constraints are those activity/event relationships which have been established as desirable but not absolutely necessary program relationships. Many such constraints normally are established in the formulation of an ideal project plan; removal of the least significant will constitute an important first step in replanning.

2. *Parallel Activities.*—Activities that are in sequential or linear order can, with the introduction of some management risk, be conducted in parallel. The decision to parallel activities will depend largely upon the availability of required resources, as well as the degree of risk that the project director considers acceptable.

3. *Eliminate Activities.*—The project may contain activities whose accomplishment might be desirable but possibly more time consuming than is permissible. If not essential, they can be eliminated.

4. *Reallocate Resources.*—The addition of resources (personnel, equipment, or material) to activities along the critical path usually will result in a reduction of activity times along this path. Thus, significant negative slack may be removed. In using this technique, a determination must be made that the time saving will justify the increased cost.

5. *Redefining Activities.*—The original plans will often contain activity descriptions that represent gross amounts of work. Careful examination of these gross activities often may reveal specific activities which can be assigned a shorter cumulative time estimate compared with the original gross activity. Further definition can take place in terms of performance levels for an activity. For example, in the case of a statistical study, a smaller sample than was originally planned might be taken.

It is important to stress that activity time estimates must not be shortened or "crashed" arbitrarily to meet a scheduled or directed date. Such a procedure would invalidate PERT as a useful management tool.

Introduction to PERT/COST

As mentioned in chapter 1, an integrated management system plans, assesses, and controls three dimensions of a program—time, cost, and performance. Up to the present, no satisfactory method has been developed which consistently integrates these three dimensions, but the establishment of PERT made a common base for such integration available. Once this was recognized, the cost dimensions of planning were rapidly introduced into the PERT system (2,8,23). The next aspect of the evolutionary development of an integrated management system,

31

based upon PERT, would be the introduction of a performance dimension into the basic system.

Principle objectives of the PERT/COST system are to aid in development of a more realistic project estimate; to compare estimated and actual costs at any selected point in the program; to help determine the best allocation of resources to project activities; and to forecast total project costs based upon program cost position throughout the project.

Cost estimates for a project should start when the work breakdown structure has been formulated, and should be based upon program elements and work packages depicted by the work breakdown structure. Although individuals activities in a network may be cost estimated, this is considered to be a burdensome and time-consuming procedure for large networks.

Figure 4, presented earlier in the chapter, illustrates the breakout of work involved in a survey project. The Instrument Development work package at Level 2 consists of the activities shown in Level 3. The relationship of this work package to the network is shown in figure 25.

Figure 25.—Relationship Between Work Package and Network Activities

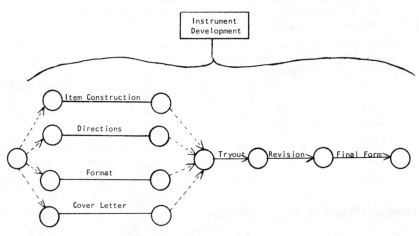

A cost estimate for the Instrument Development work package is based upon resources (personnel, equipment, material, and direct and indirect cost) needed for tasks of the succeeding tier of the work breakdown structure. These tasks are shown as activities in the network in figure 25. In order to find the total cost estimate for the project, estimates are summed from bottom to top in the work breakdown structure. Figure 26 illustrates this procedure.

Figure 26.—Summarization of Work Package Cost Estimates for Total Project Cost

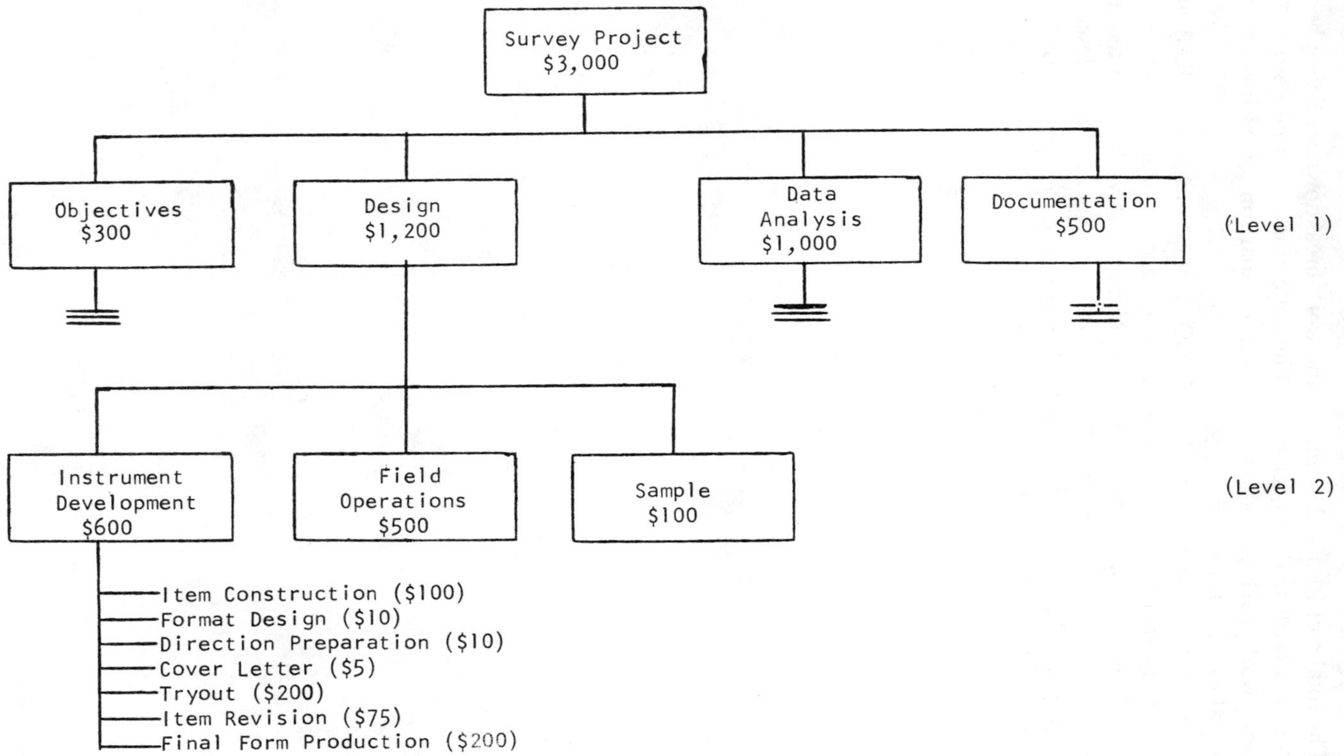

Survey Project $3,000 (Level 1)

Objectives $300

Design $1,200

Data Analysis $1,000

Documentation $500

(Level 2)

Instrument Development $600

Field Operations $500

Sample $100

Item Construction ($100)
Format Design ($10)
Direction Preparation ($10)
Cover Letter ($5)
Tryout ($200)
Item Revision ($75)
Final Form Production ($200)

33

The total cost for all elements in the work breakdown structure becomes the total estimated project cost. The collection of actual costs into the same work packages allows a direct comparison of estimated versus actual expenditures.

In addition to the basic PERT/COST application described above, two supplementary options known as *resource allocation* and *time cost* have been developed. Since these supplements have had limited actual use because of their incomplete development, an extensive description here is not appropriate, but can be found in the Department of Defense and NASA Guide for PERT/COST (8).

Chapter III
Applying PERT to Educational Research and Development Projects

PREVIOUS CHAPTERS have been devoted to a justification for using management information systems in the area of education, along with an outline of basic characteristics of the Program Evaluation and Review Technique (PERT). The purpose of this chapter is to discuss a possible application of PERT techniques to various types of educational research and development projects. The specific material to be presented consists of a general description of each type of project, along with illustrations of model work breakdown structures and networks for each application.

Categorization of various research and development activities in the field of education as to types appears not to have any degree of consistency. One approach to the problem is simply to put the several kinds of activities under two main headings—basic and applied research. More traditional categories appear in textbooks and related literature designed primarily to train students in research and development procedures. Classification of activities for this monograph follows the more traditional lines because the issue of what is basic and applied research has not been adequately resolved. The traditional approach is more readily understood by persons in the field; and such activities represent types of project activities supported by agencies such as the Cooperative Research Program of the U.S. Office of Education.

Presentation of model work breakdown structures and networks for the various kinds of projects is made with some reservation. The potential dangers inherent in using model networks as a guide for PERT applications has been well documented by Miller (16). He points out that:

> The objective of initial PERTing is to probe areas of uncertainty and discuss possible alternative paths before a final choice is made. The use of *model networks* at this point can be an aid; they may save time and provide more consistency in the overall network. However, . . . PERT is best applied to, and in fact was developed for *nonstandard situations* and that model networks should, therefore, be used with great caution.[1]

---

[1] Miller, Robert W., *Schedule, Cost, and Profit Control With PERT*. McGraw Hill Book Co., New York, 1963. p. 70.

Miller adds that the use of model networks may compromise one of the real objectives of PERT which is to obtain a network which will be valid and meaningful to the person or persons actually responsible for executing the work. Some assurance exists that in those areas for which PERT is used most effectively, no two programs are ever identical nor will two individuals have exactly the same approach to development of a network. Model networks, therefore, should be used with caution. Project directors must always be aware of the possibility of program modifications which will match the realities of their situation.

The use of such models, however, can be of value to a person who is relatively inexperienced in PERT applications. The models developed and presented in this chapter, therefore, are to serve only as guides in the application of PERT to education, and should not be considered as rigid suggestions.

Model PERT Applications

The development of models for any particular research or development activity is based on the presumption that sufficient experience with the activity exists to permit the procedural steps involved to be identified and generally agreed upon. A careful review of literature dealing with research methodologies reveals that for certain kinds of activities, such general agreement has been reached. On the other hand, certain kinds of research activities are relatively new and no adequate systematic outline of procedures has been developed to serve as a model for other researchers. For example, most procedural steps involved in organizing and conducting a survey research project have been established and are described in standard reference works available to any person undertaking such a project. The relative newness of developmental activities, however, mitigates against presentation of a model since the activity has not been performed often enough to establish a generalized procedure. Also, standard reference works on research methodology do not discuss the step involved in a developmental-type project. Agreement exists upon procedural details in certain types of research activities; these include experimental, survey, historical, curriculum, and school plant and facility studies research. Developmental projects, theory development projects, and projects concerned with integrating knowledge in a field, have not been repeated in sufficient quantity to establish a generalized procedure model, but a careful analysis of work actually done in the course of a project can lead to the development of a general list of procedural steps. An important point is that regardless of how well- or ill-defined these steps are, deviations from the generalized model are possible, depending upon the purpose and scope of a research project involving any one or combination of methods employed.

The several models presented below were developed by consulting standard reference works on research methodology, and from discussions with persons involved in the specific types of activities presented. Whenever possible, procedural steps were generalized and a model established. For those types of activities and projects where no generalized procedural outline was available, a model was developed using as a base an actual project which could be considered as representative of that particular type of activity. Each model presented below contains a descriptive categorical title, a brief explanation or definition of the type of work involved, and reference to an illustrative type of project. A model work breakdown structure is then presented in both tabular and graphic forms. A network follows, reflecting the work described at the lowest level of the work breakdown structure. In developing these models, it was recognized that some activities might well be accomplished during a proposal preparation, and hence, might be deleted from any operational work breakdown structure or network. A decision was made to include such possible steps in order to insure completeness.

Experimental Research

Experimental research is a most common activity in the field of education. The general procedure is to manipulate selected variables, using experimental and control groups, in order to study the effect of such manipulation upon selected criterion variables. Such projects may be either short or long in duration, but the steps involved are substantially the same. An example of experimentation would be an investigation designed to study the influence of vision training (corrective optical exercises) upon subsequent reading achievement.

The principal work components for this type of project, along with the work packages involved in each principal component, are presented in tabular form in figure 27 and graphically in figure 28.

One additional level has been shown under the Measurements item at Level 2 in order to demonstrate how a further subdivision might help to indicate tasks to be accomplished. A representative network for the project, presented in figure 29, shows that the formulization of objectives and hypotheses precedes development of the experimental design. In turn, once the design is developed, such activities as subject selection, procedural details, and other activities can be accomplished— many in parallel. Once the treatments have been assigned and carried out, data collection and analysis can be made. The final set of activities consists of preparing a final project report.

Figure 27.—Tabular Work Breakdown Structure for Experimental Project

LEVEL 0	LEVEL 1	LEVEL 2
Experimental Project	Problem Statement	Theoretical Framework Literature Review Objectives Hypotheses Generalization Considerations
	Design	Error Decision Treatment Definition Method of Analysis Work Guide Treatment Application Measurements
	Subjects	Sample Selection Treatment Assignment
	Analysis	Data Summary Statistical Tests Interpretation Conclusions
	Documentation	Narrative Tables Graphs Bibliography

Survey Research

Next to experimental research, survey research is probably the most common type of educational investigation. In such projects, data is collected by questionnaire and/or interview by sampling from a specified population universe in order to answer certain questions or hypotheses. Some survey research is concerned only with securing information regarding the present status of selected educational situations. Most such studies, however, are designed to secure specific information. Tabular and pictorial work breakdown structures are presented as figures 30 and 31, respectively. The representative network is presented as figure 32.

In developing the network, activities associated with establishing the hypotheses and questions regarding the study are placed first since a most common fault of such types of research is inadequate consideration of why the study is being conducted and how the data will be analyzed. After careful consideration has been given to these questions,

38

Figure 28.—Pictorial Work Breakdown Structure for Experimental Project

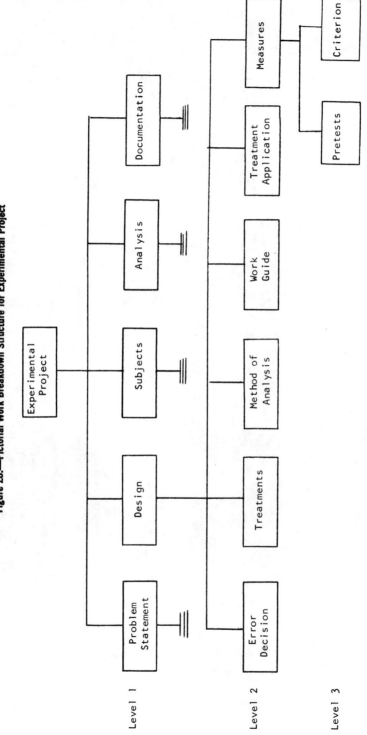

Level 1

Level 2

Level 3

39

Figure 29.—Summary Network for Experimental Research Project

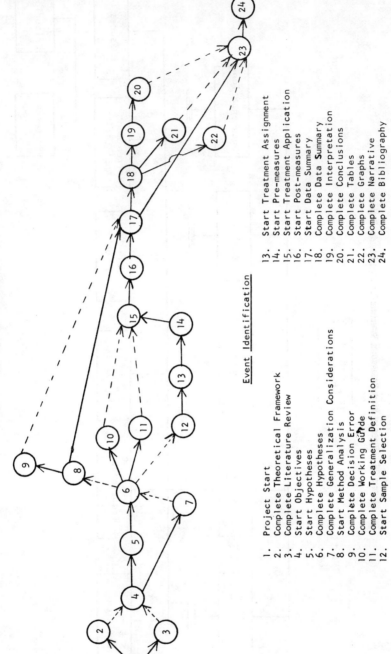

Event Identification

1. Project Start
2. Complete Theoretical Framework
3. Complete Literature Review
4. Start Objectives
5. Start Hypotheses
6. Complete Hypotheses
7. Complete Generalization Considerations
8. Start Method Analysis
9. Complete Decision Error
10. Complete Working Guide
11. Complete Treatment Definition
12. Start Sample Selection

13. Start Treatment Assignment
14. Start Pre-measures
15. Start Treatment Application
16. Start Post-measures
17. Start Data Summary
18. Complete Data Summary
19. Complete Interpretation
20. Complete Conclusions
21. Complete Tables
22. Complete Graphs
23. Complete Narrative
24. Complete Bibliography

concurrent activities in the areas of instrument construction, sample selection, and interviewer selection, can be undertaken and data collection, coding, summarization, and analysis, can be accomplished. Preparation of a final report completes the project.

Figure 30.—Tabular Work Breakdown Structure for Survey Research Project

LEVEL 1	LEVEL 2	LEVEL 3	LEVEL 4
Survey Project	Problem Statement	Objectives Data Paradigms Hypotheses	
	Design	Sample	Universe Definition Sampling Plan Sample Selection
		Instrumentation	Item Construction Tryout Form Final Form
	Data	Collection	Administrative Procedures Interview Selection Schedule Establishment Field Interviews Follow-up
		Analysis	Coding Tabulation Statistical Tests Interpretation
	Documentation	Narrative Tables Charts	

Historical Research

The general nature of historical research involves the use of existing data to answer specific questions and hypotheses. The researcher attempts to secure valid and reliable information which will lead to the acceptance or the rejection of hypotheses by a careful examination of historical records, contemporary documents, and related materials. Whenever possible, primary or original sources are utilized. A representative type of project would be one concerned with the validation of a hypothesis that the credit hour system has had strong positive influence on the organization and functions of universities.

41

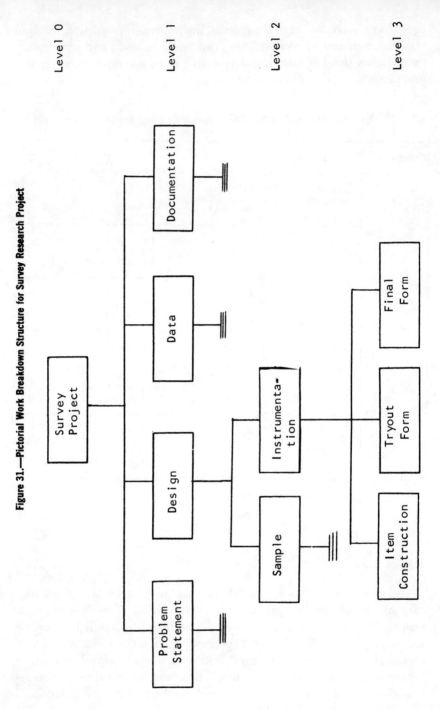

Figure 31.—Pictorial Work Breakdown Structure for Survey Research Project

Level 0

Level 1

Level 2

Level 3

Survey Project

Problem Statement

Design

Data

Documentation

Sample

Instrumentation

Item Construction

Tryout Form

Final Form

42

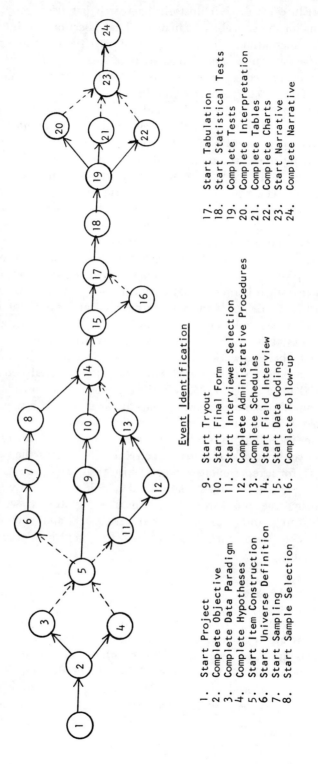

Figure 32.—Summary Network for Survey Research Project

Event Identification

1. Start Project
2. Complete Objective
3. Complete Data Paradigm
4. Complete Hypotheses
5. Start Item Construction
6. Start Universe Definition
7. Start Sampling
8. Start Sample Selection

9. Start Tryout
10. Start Final Form
11. Start Interviewer Selection
12. Complete Administrative Procedures
13. Complete Schedules
14. Start Field Interview
15. Start Data Coding
16. Complete Follow-up

17. Start Tabulation
18. Start Statistical Tests
19. Complete Tests
20. Complete Interpretation
21. Complete Tables
22. Complete Charts
23. Start Narrative
24. Complete Narrative

43

Procedure involved in historical research has been generalized into three major steps: problem statement, data collection and interpretation, and documentation. The first and third activities exist in a much more definitive pattern than does the activity of data collection and interpretation. The procedure here consists of locating primary and secondary sources and concurrently applying the concepts of external and internal criticism to the material. External criticism is concerned with determining the authenticity of a document or article, while internal criticism is concerned with evaluating the accuracy and worth of data presented. Conceivably these activities could be carried out in a linear sequence as opposed to a parallel sequence. That is, one could locate source material, abstract it, and then apply criticism to the whole. On the other hand, persons involved in historical research usually state that the processes of locating sources and applying criticism are not mutually exclusive. Since new data are constantly available to the investigator, historical research can be described as a continuous process. In a funded project, or one having some type of deadline imposed either by an investigator or external authority, the processes of locating and criticizing data sources must be terminated at some point in order to meet the scheduled completion date. For this reason, an attempt was made to establish the flow of procedures involved in such a project.

A work breakdown structure for a historical research project in tabular form appears as figure 33, with the same material being shown in pictorial form in figure 34. Within the work breakdown structure, an additional breakout of work appears at Level 3 for the item in Level 2 referred to as Source Material and Evaluation. The reason for this is to indicate that inspection and evaluation of sources probably can be best considered as concurrent activities throughout the project. The network for a representative type of historical project appears in figure 35. In general, it shows that initial activities consist of defining or delimiting the problem and establishing hypotheses, work involved in obtaining and evaluating source material, and summarizing the data, with the concluding set of activities involving document preparation.

Developmental Projects

Developmental activities as a category of research and development programs are relatively new to the field of education, although such undertakings have been carried on in military and industrial situations for many years. The basic concern is for the production of a particular kind or type of product from initial planning stages through prototypes which can then be used for production models. An illustrative case in the military field would be development of a new fighter bomber designed to meet certain specified requirements. Developmental activities of this type in the field of education are not as prevalent. Perhaps more representative types of activities in education would be the development of an instructional motion picture, a television program, or a standardized achievement test. In contrast to research activities, the sequential steps to be followed in a developmental project are not so clearly formulated, at least at the present time. It is anticipated that as educational developmental activities increase, the methodology of such projects may become more firmly established.

Figure 33.—Tabular Work Breakdown Structure for Historical Research Project

LEVEL 0	LEVEL 1	LEVEL 2	LEVEL 3
Historical Research Project	Problem Statement	Delimitation Questions and Hypotheses	
	Data Collection	Procedures	Note-Taking System Abstract Procedures Document Sources
		Source Material and Evaluation	Primary Sources Secondary Sources External Criticism Internal Criticism
		Data Summary	Interpretation Conclusions
	Documentation	Narrative Bibliography	

Because no generally agreed upon procedure exists for developmental activities, use has been made of the processes involved in development of a standardized achievement test as a representative example. The procedures involved in test development are fairly well established, and exist in standard reference works on test construction (11). Once an instrument has been developed, it can become a production-type item.

45

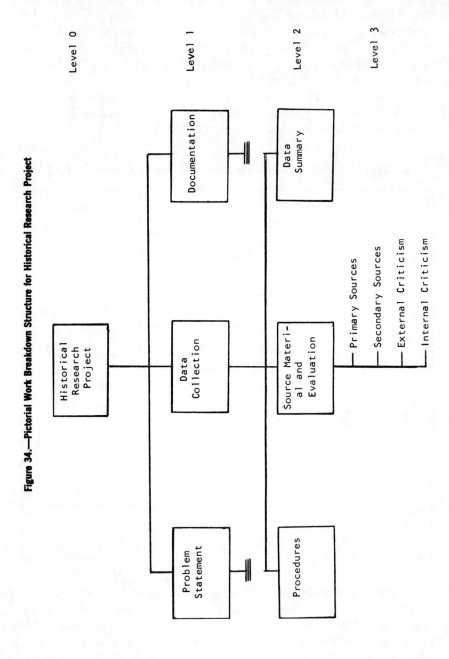

Figure 34.—Pictorial Work Breakdown Structure for Historical Research Project

46

Figure 35.—Summary Network for Historical Research Project

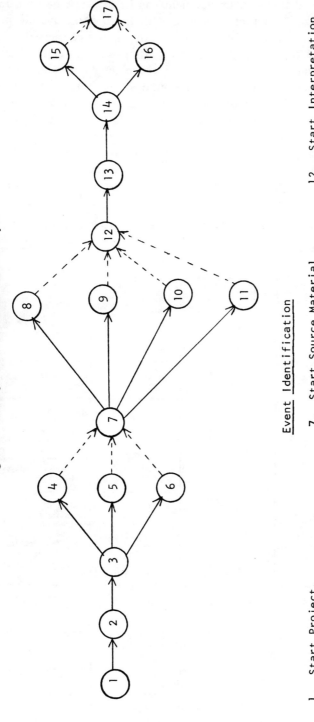

Event Identification

1. Start Project
2. Complete Problem Statement
3. Complete Question and Hypotheses
4. Complete Note System
5. Complete Abstract System
6. Complete Document Sources Identify

7. Start Source Material and Evaluation
8. Complete Primary Sources
9. Complete Secondary Sources
10. Complete External Criticism
11. Complete Internal Criticism

12. Start Interpretation
13. Start Conclusion
14. Complete Conclusions
15. Complete Narrative
16. Complete Bibliography
17. Project End

47

The general end items of development consist of a test booklet and accessory material. Activities associated with the booklet include preparing a test plan consisting of the purpose and nature of the test, item construction and tryout, final form preparation, and normative data. Accessory materials to accompany the test booklet consists of answer sheets, administrative directions, and similar items. The test booklet and accessory material preparation comprise Level (1) of the tabular work breakdown structure shown in figure 36. The major end item of a test booklet is further broken down into the preparation of a test plan, the creation of an item pool, plus the development of tryout and final forms of the test. Accessory materials consist of the manual containing pertinent test information and answer sheets to be used, along with a

Figure 36.—Tabular Work Breakdown Structure for Achievement Test Development Project

LEVEL 0	LEVEL 1	LEVEL 2	LEVEL 3	LEVEL 4
Achievement Test	Test Booklet	Test Plan	Purpose Objectives Content Specifications	
		Item Pool	Item Writers	
			Test Items	Item Drafts Item Review
		Test Forms	Tryout Forms	Student Directions Administration Directions Tryout Sample Form Assembly Tryout Administration Statistical Analysis Revised Item
			Final Form	Student Directions Administration Directions Norm Sample Final Test Booklet Norm Administration Statistical Analysis Normative Data
	Accessory Material	Manual	Outline Preliminary Draft Final Draft	
		Answer Sheets	Machine-Score Hand-Score	
		Scoring Procedure	Keys Directions	

48

scoring procedure. Succeeding levels of the work breakdown structure show further detail work under each of the Level (3) subdivisions. A pictorial presentation of the work breakdown structure occurs in figure 37. The network for a test development project following the above work breakdown structure is presented as figure 38.

The first set of activities involves establishing the test's purpose and specifications, followed by preparation of an outline showing the subject, objectives, and content to be covered. These latter two activities are shown here as being in parallel, but quite possibly they might be considered by some persons as a single activity. Once the test plan has been prepared, item writers can be employed. The preparation of item drafts and their review can be carried out as concurrent activities, after which several activities can be carried on at the same time. Student and administrator directions can be prepared, the tryout sample selected, the answer sheet prepared, and scoring procedures established. The fact should be noted that the sampling plan to be followed in selecting both tryout and norm samples can be started once specifications for the test are known. When this set of activities has been accomplished, the tryout administration can take place, followed by statistical analysis and item revision. An outline of the manual can also begin as soon as materials have been assembled from the tryout.

Upon completion of item revision, the final test form may be assembled. Experience gained in the tryout administration can be used to revise student and administrator directions. The final norming sample is selected following the sampling plan established by the tryout sample. Upon accomplishment of these activities, the normative administration can be made, followed by a statistical analysis of the test data and establishment of desired normative data. While the above activities are being carried out, a preliminary draft of the manual may be prepared, but its final form cannot be accomplished until normative data are available from the final test administration. The project can be considered finished when both the test booklet and the accessory material are completed.

Curriculum Development

The development of curricula and accompanying instructional materials is a continuous process in the field of education. Consequently, the steps involved in developing a new curriculum unit or revising an existing one have been fairly well established. Curriculum development can take place as a joint teacher-student activity in a particular subject area throughout the semester, or it can take the form of a resource unit

50

Figure 37.—Pictorial Work Breakdown Structure for Achievement Test Development Project

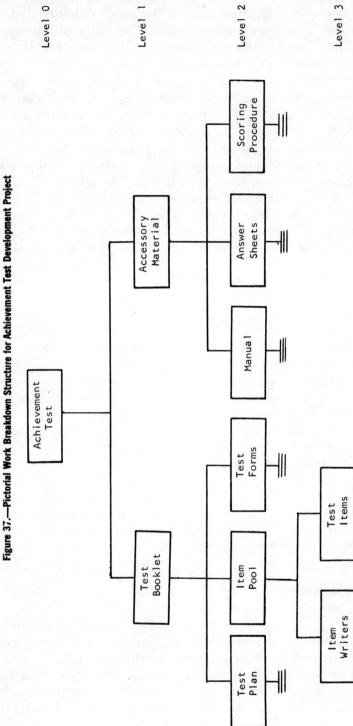

Level 0

Level 1

Level 2

Level 3

Figure 38.—Summary Network for Achievement Test Development Project

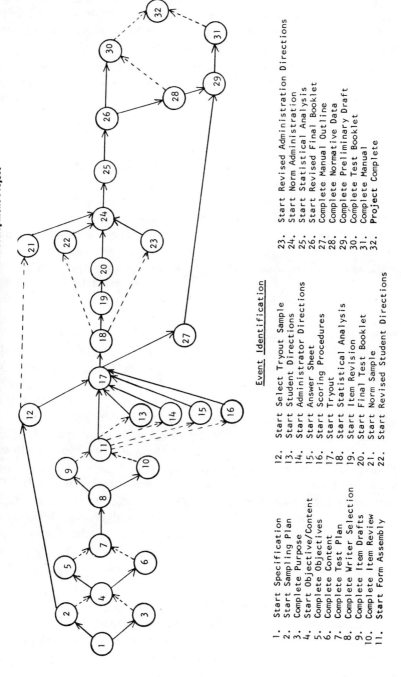

Event Identification

1. Start Specification
2. Start Sampling Plan
3. Complete Purpose
4. Start Objective/Content
5. Complete Objectives
6. Complete Content
7. Complete Test Plan
8. Complete Writer Selection
9. Complete Item Drafts
10. Complete Item Review
11. Start Form Assembly

12. Start Select Tryout Sample
13. Start Student Directions
14. Start Administrator Directions
15. Start Answer Sheet
16. Start Scoring Procedures
17. Start Tryout
18. Start Statistical Analysis
19. Start Item Revision
20. Start Final Test Booklet
21. Start Norm Sample
22. Start Revised Student Directions

23. Start Revised Administration Directions
24. Start Norm Administration
25. Start Statistical Analysis
26. Start Revised Final Booklet
27. Complete Manual Outline
28. Complete Normative Data
29. Complete Preliminary Draft
30. Complete Test Booklet
31. Complete Manual
32. Project Complete

51

made available to teachers as needed. A curriculum can be developed on a national scale as witnessed by projects such as the SMSG Mathematics Program, the Physical Science Study Committee, Project English, and similar programs. On the other hand, local school districts often undertake their own curriculum development activities.

The principal goal of a curriculum development project is to provide the teacher with a rather complete package of instructional materials, including an orientation to their development and use. Thus, it is possible to say that two major work activities constitute the production of a curriculum. One major activity is concerned with development and preparation of instructional materials and the other with the process of disseminating information about these materials.

The preparation of instructional materials consists of work centering around determining instructional goals and evaluating them from several points of view, plus establishing the structure to be used in organizing knowledge in the subject field. Once objectives and structure have been determined, initial material development can begin. Identifiable work units revolve around teacher and student materials, audio-visual materials, evaluation techniques, and additional reference material. After initial materials have been developed, they are subjected to a field test or tryout in a selected sample of schools. Upon completion of these operations, final instructional material can be prepared.

The dissemination process can begin early in a project by outlining the necessary procedures and by selecting schools before all material is ready. When the final materials are available, teachers and administrators can be oriented to their nature and use. Lay personnel such as PTA groups can be oriented once the school staff understands the material.

The tabular work breakdown structure appearing in figure 39 identifies work units within the two major work areas. The pictorial illustration of this work breakdown appearing in figure 40 shows only those work units comprising the work area labeled Initial Materials. The network for a curriculum project shown in figure 41 indicates that determination of objectives and structure could be considered as occurring concurrently along with some aspects of the dissemination process being initiated at the project starting point. Once goals and structure have been established, the material can be prepared. Upon completion of the field test, final materials can be shown as being in the development stage. In turn, the preparation of publications, reports, and manuals can be shown to constrain the orientation of teachers, administrators, and lay personnel. A desirable innovation might be to include some further activities associated with feedback possibly obtained from the dissemination-orientation phase.

Figure 39.—Tabular Work Breakdown Structure for Curriculum Project

LEVEL 0	LEVEL 1	LEVEL 2	LEVEL 3	LEVEL 4
Resource Unit	Material Preparation	Objectives	Goals	Philosophical Evaluation Psychological Evaluation Content Evaluation Measurement Evaluation
			Structure	Determination Evaluation
		Instructional Materials	Initial Material	Teacher Material Student Material Audiovisual Aids Evaluation Techniques Reference Material
			Field Test	Procedures School Sample Material Distribution Tryout Evaluation
			Final Material	Revised Teacher Material Revised Student Material
	Dissemination	Publication	Texts Manuals Reports	
		Orientation	Teachers Administrators Lay Personnel	

Educational Service Projects

A major activity in the field of education is the planning of comprehensive educational programs, including both the instructional program and school plant and facilities. Because comprehensive planning may be beyond the competency of a local school district, contractual arrangements can often be made with such other agencies as university research and service bureaus, to assist local school personnel in developing all or part of a plan. Such arrangements usually exist between local school districts and the consulting agency, but not uncommonly, they may exist on a state or regional basis. Since the essential nature of this activity is to provide a service to the local school district, those general types of activities involved have been categorized as educational service activities. Representative types in this category would be school enrollment projection surveys, curriculum evaluation projects, space determination and utilization projects, and similar ac-

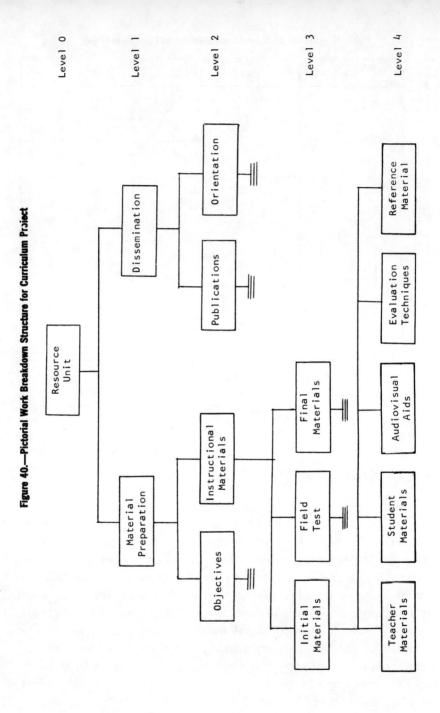

Figure 40.—Pictorial Work Breakdown Structure for Curriculum Project

Level 0

Level 1

Level 2

Level 3

Level 4

Resource Unit

Dissemination

Orientation

Publications

Material Preparation

Instructional Materials

Objectives

Final Materials

Field Test

Initial Materials

Reference Material

Evaluation Techniques

Audiovisual Aids

Student Materials

Teacher Materials

54

Figure 41.—Summary Network for Curriculum Project

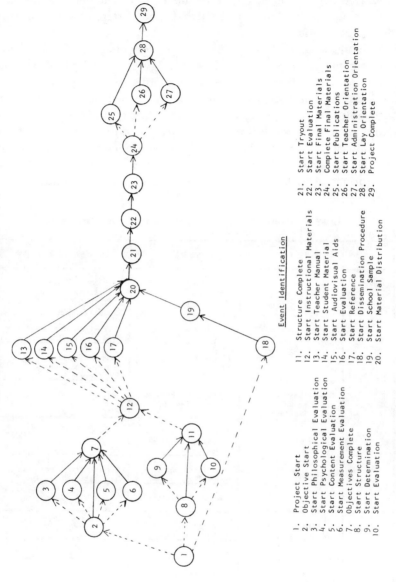

Event Identification

1. Project Start
2. Objective Start
3. Start Philosophical Evaluation
4. Start Psychological Evaluation
5. Start Content Evaluation
6. Start Measurement Evaluation
7. Objectives Complete
8. Start Structure
9. Start Determination
10. Start Evaluation

11. Structure Complete
12. Start Instructional Materials
13. Start Teacher Manual
14. Start Student Material
15. Start Audiovisual Aids
16. Start Evaluation
17. Start Reference
18. Start Dissemination Procedure
19. Start School Sample
20. Start Material Distribution

21. Start Tryout
22. Start Evaluation
23. Start Final Materials
24. Complete Final Materials
25. Start Publications
26. Start Teacher Orientation
27. Start Administration Orientation
28. Start Lay Orientation
29. Project Complete

55

tivities. One of the most common types consists of planning the school plant, and generalized steps involved have been described in the National Council on School House Construction Guide (18). To illustrate a possible application of PERT to this type of situation, the model in this section was developed from a description of steps involved in school plant programing.

Activities associated with school plant designing can be subdivided into four major work areas as shown in figures 42 and 43. First, a district-wide plant survey should be made in order to develop a master plan for future school district construction, after which specifications could be established for buildings within the district. These specifications would serve as a guide for architectural planning, design, and construction of buildings. The provision of equipment and actual occupation of the new building would complete these activities. Detailed descriptions of each step are provided in the above reference.

Figure 42.—Tabular Work Breakdown Structure for School Plant Project

LEVEL 0	LEVEL 1	LEVEL 2	LEVEL 3
School Plant Program	District-Wide Plant Survey	Determination of Present and Future Needs	Enrollment Projections Educational Program Projections Summary of Needs
		Existing Resource Survey	Current Plant Appraisal Finance and Planning Report
		Recommended Plan	Long-Range Plans Short-Range Plans Immediate Plans
	Educational Building Specifications	Educational Program Planning Review	
		Teaching-Station and Space Requirements	
		Specifications Guide	Quantitative Dimensions Qualitative Dimensions
		Review Architectural Plan	
	Architectural Plans and Construction	Architect Employment	Selection Services
		Construction	
	Employment and Occupancy	Furniture and Equipment Selection	
		Teacher-Student Orientation	
		Document File	
		Public Relations	

Figure 43.—Pictorial Work Breakdown Structure for School Plant Project

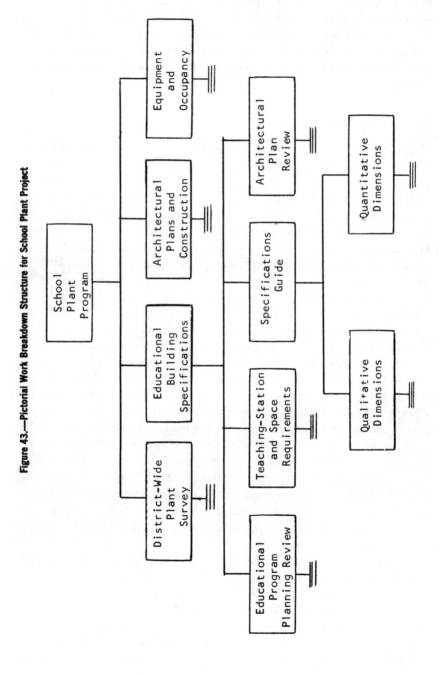

Model work breakdown structures presented in this section, therefore, probably should be considered as representing major work units. The network shown in figure 44 shows only the major activities to be accomplished, and thus should be considered as a summary rather than a detailed network for this type of project. Detailed networks could be established to show a plan for actual work involved in the construction phase or any other aspect of the plan where management control is essential.

Research Integration Project

An often-stated criticism of educational research is that although much has been accomplished, systematic efforts to integrate this research have been neglected. Therefore, it cannot always serve as a foundation for instructional procedures and/or as a guideline for new research programs to cover areas not adequately investigated. Recent recognition has been given to this situation by the U.S. Office of Education Cooperative Research Program which now considers the conduct of research integration studies as significant and worthy of financial support.

This type of project involves a systematic review of unpublished and published research in a defined area for the purpose of establishing a set of educational principles, to formulate a theory which can then be used as a guide for developing current educational practices, or to determine the present state of research. An example of such a project would be a systematic review of research literature relating to the field of music education conducted at The Ohio State University under a grant from the Cooperative Research Program (21). The particular goal of this project was not to establish a list of instructional principles for music education, but to establish the areas in music education which have been researched and those which still need attention. The outline below represents a generalized model for this type of research, derived largely from experience gained in conducting such an activity by personnel from the music education research synthesis project. It is important, therefore, to recognize that a similar project might deviate from the model in some aspects.

The general work to be done in such a project is to establish a procedure for evaluating the research, followed by activities associated with collecting the data (in this case research documents), developing a system for classifying the research, and then conducting an integration and synthesis of research findings.

A tabular work breakdown structure for such a project is presented in figure 45 with a pictorial illustration of the same structure given as

Figure 44.—Summary Network for School Plant Project

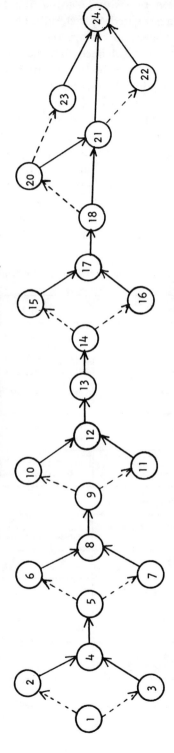

Event Identification

1. Project Start
2. Start Enrollment Projections
3. Start Educational Program Projections
4. Start Needs Summary
5. Complete Needs Summary
6. Start Plant Appraisal
7. Start Finance Report
8. Start Long Range Plan
9. Complete Long Range Plan
10. Start Immediate Plan
11. Start Short Range Report
12. Start Educational Program Planning Review
13. Start Teaching-Station and Space Requirements
14. Start Specifications Guide
15. Start Quantitative Dimensions
16. Start Qualitative Dimensions
17. Complete Specification Guide
18. Complete Architectural Arrangements
19. Complete Construction
20. Start Furniture and Equipment Selection
21. Complete Construction
22. Start Public Relations
23. Start Document File
24. Complete Teacher-Student Orientation

figure 46. The research evaluation procedure consists of establishing a definition of the field to be investigated by determining what will be considered to be research and what topics are relevant to the investigation, after which the field can be defined. Development of an evaluation instrument is based upon a review of existing techniques followed by construction of a format for abstracting and evaluating the research. Data collection consists primarily of compiling an initial list of studies appearing in published literature as well as determining their existence in unpublished form. Once the research reports have been identified, activities are undertaken to procure necessary documents by use of interlibrary loan facilities, microfilm purchase, and similar sources, and when the material has been received, abstracts can be prepared. Activities involved in data collection are conducted largely in parallel. That is, the procurement and abstraction could constitute an on-going process until the project staff feels that it should

Figure 45.—Tabular Work Breakdown Structure for Research Integration Project

LEVEL 0	LEVEL 1	LEVEL 2	LEVEL 3
Research Synthesis Report	Research Evaluation Procedures	Definition of Field	Relevancy Definition Research Definition
		Evaluation Instrument Development	Review of Research Evaluation Technique Research Abstraction and Evaluation Form
	Data Collection	Bibliographic Listing	Published Material Unpublished Material
		Research Report Procurement	Microfilms Inter-Library Loan
		Abstract Preparation	
	Category Development	Preliminary Form	Logical Consideration Philosophical Considerations
		Final Form	
		Abstract Assignment	
	Research Synthesis and Integration	Synthesis of Research Findings	1. Data Collection 2. "Like" Studies Summary
		Recommendation for Future Research	
		Annotated Bibliography	

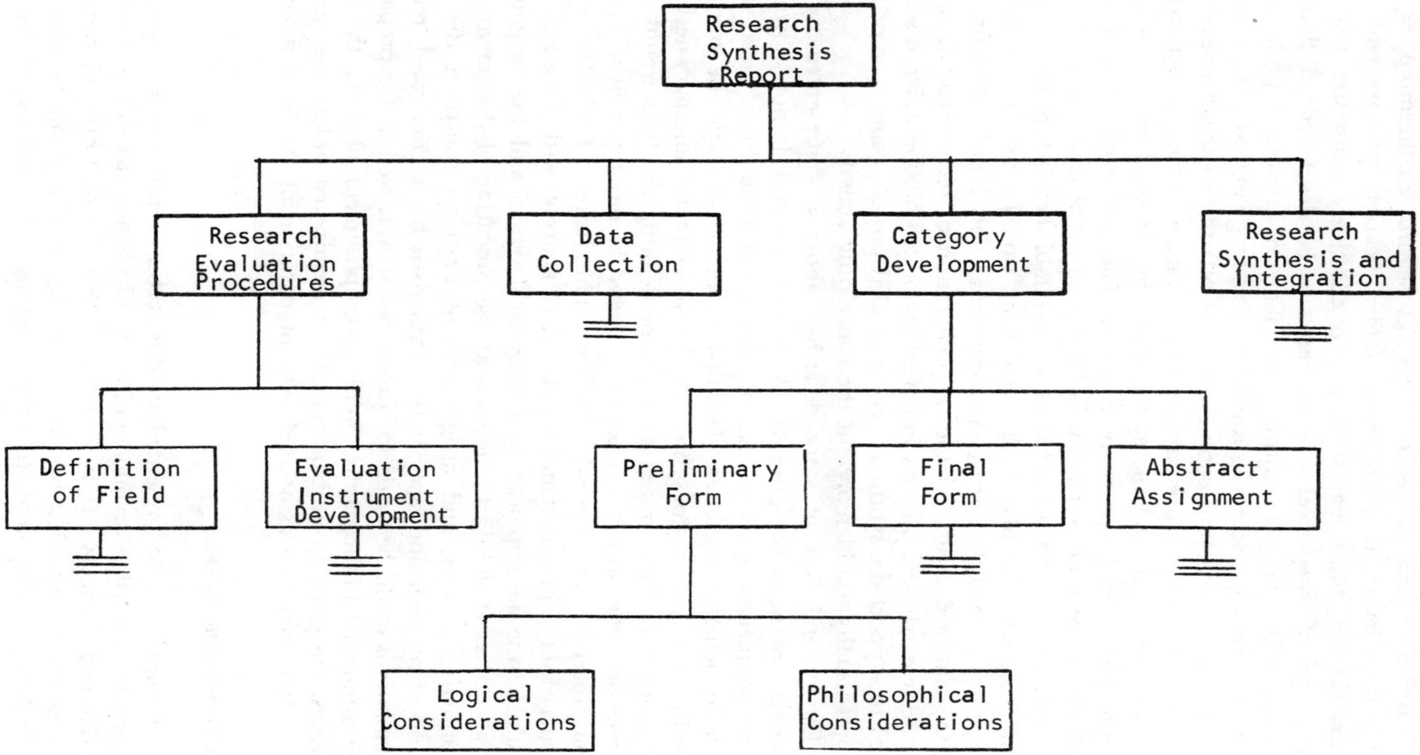

Figure 46.—Pictorial Work Breakdown Structure for Research Integration Project

be terminated and succeeding activities begun. Furthermore, as one study is reviewed, it often leads to identification, procurement, and abstraction of additional studies. To effectively synthesize research, some type of categorical scheme needs to be developed so that the studies can be arranged according to variables of interest. A preliminary form or outline of categories can be derived by giving careful consideration to logical and philosophical aspects relating to the defined field. After a review of this preliminary categorization scheme, a final system can be established, and thereafter, abstracts prepared in the data collection phase can be properly assigned. The nature of this activity is such that once a project is initiated, development of a categorical system can begin, but it would have to be established before the research synthesis could take place. The final work would consist of a synthesis and integration of the research to consist of an anlysis of research findings in the classified areas and topics, preparation of recommendations for future research, and preparation of an annotated bibliography of studies used to support the synthesis. For a funded project, some type of final report usually would represent the concluding activity.

The general flow of work described above is represented by the summary network in figure 47. A detailed network is not shown because uniqueness of such types of projects would no doubt cause variation in actual procedures. Detailed subnetworks could be outlined also for each of the major gross activities shown on the summary network. As represented here, initial activities of defining the field would commence once the project was begun, followed by development of evaluation procedures and the initial bibliographic listing. Thereafter, documents could be procured and abstracted. Concurrent with these activities could be the development of a categorical system and the assignment of abstracts. It should be noted that the procuring of documents, the abstracting process, and assignments of abstracts constrain the synthesis of research findings. As the synthesis is being conducted, recommendations could be made for future research as well as for preparing the annotated bibliography. With accomplishment of these three activities, the project could be considered terminated unless one desired to include activities associated with preparation of the final report.

Theory Development Project

The model to be presented in this section represents a project designed to establish a taxonomy of observed phenomena as a first step in developing a theory. It is anticipated that the outlining of steps involved in such a project would be of value for other projects concerned with theory development, (i.e., the collecting and classifying of observed

Figure 47.—Summary Network for Research Integration Project

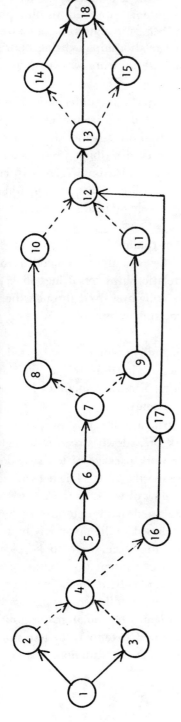

Event Identification

1. Project Start
2. Complete Relevancy Definition
3. Complete Research Definition
4. Start Evaluation Instrument
5. Complete Research Evaluation Instrument Review
6. Complete Abstract and Evaluation Form
7. Complete Initial Bibliography List
8. Start Procurement
9. Start Abstracting

10. Complete Procurement
11. Complete Abstracting
12. Start Abstract Assignment
13. Start Synthesis and Integration
14. Start Recommendations for Future Research
15. Start Annotated Bibliography
16. Start Preliminary Category Development
17. Start Final Category Development
18. Project Complete

phenomena). Specifically, the model presented represents work done in connection with attempts to establish a taxonomy of teacher-classroom behavior (7). The author's intent, as stated in the proposal, was to observe teacher-classroom behavior patterns, organize them systematically in order to determine relationships existing between the observed elements, and then to establish a theory which could later be subjected to verification.

To achieve the first goal, three major work units were identified—establish types of data to be collected by reviewing existing teacher behavior classification schemes as well as schemes for other social process areas; prepare a working paper describing these taxonomies; submit this to experts for comment and distribute these written comments to other interested reviewers for study. This process, when completed, would lead to a synthesizing of a single taxonomy and a resultant paradigm.

The method here would consist of conducting a seminar for further consolidation of the taxonomies; these would be extended to cover gaps by observing logical interrelationships resulting in a single taxonomy, and an accompanying paradigm evolved through the identification of variables to be included, and by providing working or operational definitions for each.

The completed taxonomy and paradigm would be subjected to empirical tests by using them in a series of filmed as well as live classroom situations. From these two activities, necessary modifications and revision would be made in the final taxonomy.

The tabular work breakdown structure for this project is shown as figure 48, and the pictorial work breakdown structure as figure 49. In the latter, only the intermediate work package of test situations has been further broken down into more specific units. The network is given in summary form as figure 50. The flow of work, as represented by this network, shows that activities associated with determining types of teacher behavior, which might be included in the taxonomy by a review of existing educational and related literature, were to be completed first, followed by a review by experts of existent taxonomies. Development of the synthesized taxonomy and paradigm, including the seminar which is held for face-to-face discussion, is followed by the synthesized taxonomy and accompanying paradigm. The final major unit work will consist of subjecting the synthesized taxonomy to test situations. In consequence of results obtained in the test situation, this taxonomy would then be modified and revised.

Figure 48.—Tabular Work Breakdown Structure for Teacher Behavior Taxonomy Project

LEVEL 0	LEVEL 1	LEVEL 2	LEVEL 3
Teacher Classroom Behavior Taxonomy	Teacher-Behavior Data Analysis	Working Paper on Taxonomies	Review of Teacher Behavior Systems Review of Social Process Fields
		Working Paper Review	Expert Selection Working Paper Distribution Expert Review Distribution of Reaction Papers
	Taxonomy and Paradigm Development	Review Seminar	Seminar Plans Seminar Seminar Summary
		Synthesized Taxonomy	Extension of Taxonomies Logical Interrelationships
		Paradigm Development	Variable Identification Variable Definitions
	Taxonomy Test and Modification	Test	Observations Facilities Film Observation Classroom Observation
		Modification	Assess Film Reports Assess Classroom Reports

Further Applications of PERT

It should be kept in mind that the work breakdown structures and networks presented in this chapter are only illustrative and therefore should not be considered as rigid statements of the work to be done. Additional levels could be added to any of the work breakdown structures to cope with further detail work. The configuration and content of a project's work breakdown, and the specific work packages to be identified, vary depending upon such considerations as the (1) size and complexity of the project, (2) time available for planning, (3) degree of uncertainty involved, (4) project director's judgment of work assignments, and (5) structure of the various organizations concerned. Once established, a work breakdown structure must be maintained and updated to reflect any changing situations. In this chapter also, no attempt was made to illustrate time estimates involved in doing the several activities since the specific nature of each research and development project would necessitate its own peculiar time estimates. As experience is

Figure 49.—Pictorial Work Breakdown Structure for Teacher Behavior Taxonomy Project

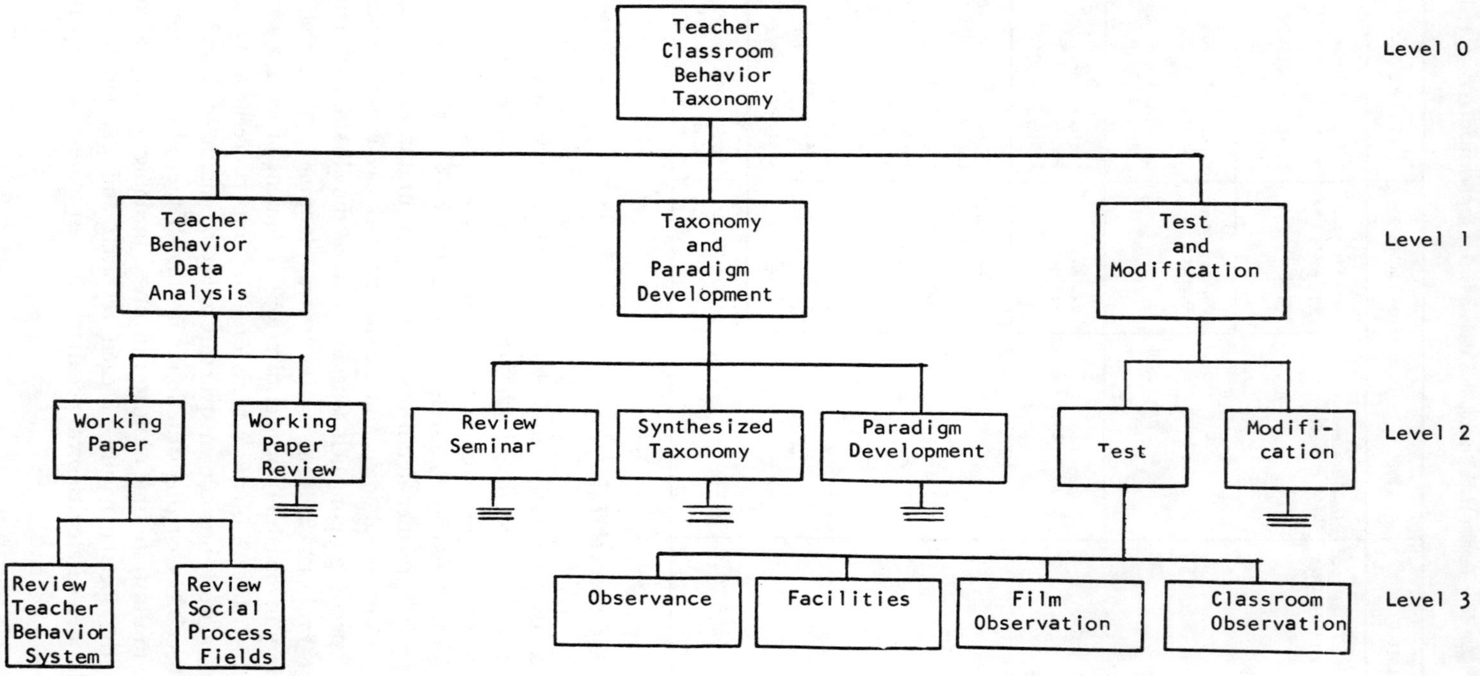

Figure 50.—Summary Network for Teacher Behavior Taxonomy Project

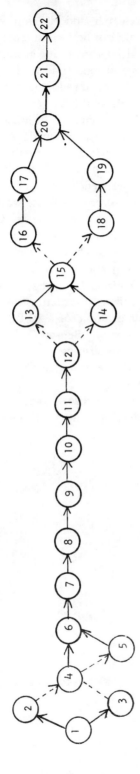

Event Identification

1. Project Start
2. Complete Review of Existing Taxonomies
3. Complete Review of Social Process Fields
4. Start Working Paper
5. Start Selection of Review Experts
6. Start Distribution of Working Papers
7. Start Expert Review of Working Paper
8. Start Duplication of Experts' Reactions
9. Complete Expert Review
10. Complete Seminar
11. Complete Taxonomy Synthesis

12. Complete Paradigm
13. Start Observer Selection
14. Start Facilities Arrangements
15. Start Test Situations
16. Start Film Observations
17. Start Film Assessment
18. Start Classroom Observation
19. Start Classroom Assessment
20. Start Modification and Review
21. Start Final Report
22. Project Complete

67

gained in managing educational research and development projects through the use of PERT, perhaps data can be accumulated with regard to the time required to complete activities, thus giving grounds for better estimates of individual activity times and total time for future projects.

In addition to the types of research and development activities presented in this chapter, possibly models could be generated for other kinds of research activity. For example, a common illustration would be the prediction studies where extensive use has been made of correlational analysis, as in the case of academic performance prediction studies. Another common research activity is *ex post facto* studies where the investigator collects data in terms of selected hypotheses and questions and analyzes the relationships existing in his data to see whether certain conditions existing prior to collection could cause the relationships.

At this time, the reader should note that educational applications of PERT are not restricted solely to research and development. The system can and has been used in project-type situations such as developing and establishing a junior college, installing a computer system for a school district, and reorganizing an administrative structure at the university level. An excellent example of a PERT application in the junior college field is the work done by Benson (5) in determining the sequence of activities involved in establishing a new junior college. Such types of projects usually meet the several criteria for PERT implementation as outlined in chapter 4.

Management specialists in general recognize, however, that PERT is most suitable for research and development activities and not for routine or production-type projects.

Chapter IV

Implementing PERT on Educational Research and Development Projects

THE PURPOSE OF THIS CHAPTER is to outline some practical considerations regarding the actual implementation of PERT. All contingencies cannot be covered but some guidelines derived from practical experience will help to facilitate the process.

Decision as to Adoption of PERT

The PERT technique can be applied to almost any project where logical planning is required. Applications can be made to a one-man project or to one involving many persons, institutions, or agencies. The decision regarding use of PERT should be made on the basis of several criteria.

First, does a specified end objective exist, the accomplishment of which can be determined? Repetitious activities, such as student registration procedures, are not the kinds of projects for which PERT is most useful. A project designed to develop a new registration procedure, to be ready by a certain date, would be a more typical application. Some benefit can be derived from applying PERT to repetitive processes in order to determine the most efficient mode of operation. For example, registration procedures might be diagramed or networked to determine whether the optimum logic or sequence is being developed. An application of this type is illustrated in a study on registration procedures of Syracuse University, reported by Smith (22).

Second, must some scheduled date or deadline be met? If no particular need exists to reach an end objective on schedule, one need not be concerned with time management. Projects funded by agencies having definite directed completion dates are most suitable for PERT application.

Third, what is the degree of project complexity? It is difficult to indicate exactly how complex a project should be before implementing PERT, but in general, those involving one or two persons over a period of approximately 2 months, with a network consisting of perhaps 20 to 25 events, might represent a minimum complexity. No firm objective

69

standards have been set, however, for this criterion. As the complexity of a project increases, the need for PERT grows.

Fourth, does a degree of uncertainty exist as to the definition of some or all program elements? If the project possesses the "once-through" characteristic, PERT will be quite applicable. If the project, however, is rather routine and standardized and much experience exists with regard to operations and time sequences, PERT probably is unnecessary. In some cases, PERT might be used in initial research and development stages, and after production-type items have been developed another management system might be employed to plan and control the operation.

An additional consideration as to whether or not PERT can be applied or implemented effectively on a project must relate to experiences of project managers and other personnel with PERT. Agencies utilizing this system do so in different ways; some have technical PERT specialists functioning in a staff capacity to assist in all operations except decision-making; others train line personnel. In any case, project personnel should have an adequate orientation before trying to employ PERT. A minimum orientation would consist of approximately 8 hours of lecture and practical work. A PERT specialist would be helpful in the early stages of implementation.

Time of Implementation

The original development of PERT concentrated upon its use as a technique for ascertaining the progress of a project or program as is indicated by its title, Program Evaluation and Review Technique. During implementation of the original process, it became apparent that the technique had value as a tool in planning projects during the program definition or proposal preparation phases. Consequently, it is being employed more and more for both functions.

It is highly recommended, therefore, that the concepts and principles of PERT be utilized during the process of preparing research and development proposals before their submission to a funding agency. The value of such an application lies not only in deriving a time schedule for the project, but more importantly, it can serve as a method for checking the logic as well as identifying necessary activities of the plan along with their sequence and dependency. A review of reasons for project proposal rejection would reveal that a large proportion are not funded because of inadequate description of procedures to be carried out. This usually means that insufficient prior attention was given to techniques and procedures to be utilized in conducting the research.

70

Careful planning of a research project requires considerable time. In fact, planning a research and development project may require more time than the research work itself.

Construction of a work breakdown structure and a correlated network during early stages of project planning is of value in that they can identify program elements that might be overlooked. They can also determine the sequence of work and constraints imposed upon subsequent projects by the.completion of earlier activities. They would serve as valuable communication tools to the person reviewing a proposal for funding. Communicating project processes through use of a network can quickly convey the plan's logic and whether the researcher has considered necessary interrelationships. Furthermore, end products would be more readily identified. Usually they take the form of a final report, but not unusually, these final end items consist of curriculum guides, instructional films, textbooks, or similar items.

One should not be too concerned that network establishment in the planning stages of a project would result in freezing the work and thus inhibit the investigation of promising leads which might develop during the project. It is important to understand that PERT is a dynamic system. That is, any research and/or development project probably will not progress exactly according to plan, and changes may occur both in the final end item and in the process of arriving at this goal. As a project progresses, work breakdown structures and networks can be supplemented to accommodate program changes provided they will not result in an overrun of total project cost in a fixed price contract situation nor seriously modify the final end item. Such major program redefinitions usually must be cleared by the funding agency before being incorporated into the project framework.

Network Construction

As noted in chapter 2, the network is the basic feature of the PERT technique. It portrays graphically the tasks to be done, the order in which they are to be undertaken, and it serves as a communication tool for other staff members. It is important, therefore, that the network be carefully drawn, especially since this operation demands constant revision and changes. Simplified procedures for establishing the first or original network should be employed. Experience has shown that using large sheets of newsprint, blackboard, or large sheets of acetate-covered cardboard and grease pencil are useful techniques. Engineering fade-out vellum is an ideal paper. PERT templates also facilitate networking. The employment of "activity" cards in preparation of networks also is helpful. This procedure consists of identifying each project activity on a separate 3" x 5" card. The cards are then distributed on a large table, working backward from end objective to project start. They can be moved about freely in order to insure the establishment of proper dependencies and interrelationships. When the final placement of cards has been made, a hand copy of the network can be prepared, using the cards as activity lines and putting event circles at start and end points. After the network is drawn, the events can be numbered and these numbers placed on the original activity card. If the additional step of time estimating is taken at this time, that information also can be added to the network as well as to the cards. An activity card such as that shown in figure 51 could be used as a source document for keypunching since it would contain the basic information needed for most computer programs. The possible presence of many crossing lines and other conditions which might disfigure the initial network should not be a source of discouragement since the network can be redesigned.

Figure 51.—Sample Activity Card

```
PRED. EVENT NO._____          SUCC. EVENT NO._____


ACTIVITY_____


    Optimistic time (a)                    _____

    Most likely time (m)                   _____

    Pessimistic time (b)                   _____

    Expected elapsed time (t_e)            _____


            (See Reverse Side for Detailed Description)
```

Network Processing

The processing of network computations in order to arrive at such information as Expected Elapsed Time, Earliest Expected Date, Latest Allowable Date, and Slack, can be done either manually or by a computer. Manual procedures consist of using such devices as nomographs, circular slide rules, and/or desk calculators. Nomographs and slide rules are available at a nominal cost and can be useful in calculating Expected Elapsed Time or t_e. The calculation of T_E and T_L, which are essentially summation and subtraction processes, can be done on a desk calculator. No definite network size has been established with regard to the practicality of hand computations. A consensus seems to indicate that a network of 200 events or less can be handled satisfactorily by manual procedures. Networks larger than this usually are handled by data processing techniques.

Numerous computer programs have been written for PERT computations by agencies using the system as well as by companies producing computers. A comprehensive listing of PERT computer programs, along with their individual characteristics, appears in a document by Phillips and Beek (20). In addition to network size, another reason for using the computer is that desired information can be obtained quickly and accurately. The general input data for computer processing consists of the following items:

A. Predecessor and successor event numbers.
B. Activity descriptions.
C. One or three time estimates.
D. Schedule and/or directed dates.
E. Milestone event designation.
F. Desired sorts (critical path report, etc.).

An input data sheet for the U.S. Air Force PERT computer program is presented as figure 52. It should be pointed out that some computer programs require that the event numbers be in sequential order while others take a random number sequence. A prospective user of a PERT computer program should examine it carefully to determine its particular characteristics and the exact nature of input data requirements.

The general output from the several computer programs varies according to characteristics peculiar to the program. Most computer programs are designed to perform the activities of calculating average or Expected Elapsed Time, Earliest Expected Dates, and Latest Allowable Dates, along with Critical and limit paths. Consequently, many kinds of reports are available. A useful one is the "audit list" which is a complete listing of all events and activities comprising the network. Checking this report against the original network will insure that all activities and related information have been recorded carefully. Additional reports can be secured that list events and activities by their Latest Allowable Date, Earliest Expected Date, and Slack. Some programs print out all network paths with accompanying Slack, while others have the option of selecting only the Critical Path. Some programs also have a feature which allows a report to be generated listing activities assigned to a particular division or unit. Such a report is sometimes referred to as an Organization or Responsibility Report. If the program

Figure 52.—U.S. Air Force PERT Time Input Form

PERT TIME INPUT FORM

INITIAL CARD

REPORT DATE			RUN NO	BLANK	BLANK	MASTER FILE	NETWORK START DATE			E–L CHART	SUMMARY	EVENT OUTPUT	BLANK	RUN DATE	BLANK	NETWORK COMPLETION DATE			SYSTEM OR PROJECT NUMBER						
DAY	MO	YR					MO	DAY	YR							MO	DAY	YR							
1	2 3	4 5	6 7	8 9	10	11	12	13 14	15 16 17	18 19	20 21	22	23	24	25 26	27 28 29	30 31	32	33 34 35 36	37 38	39 40	41 42	43			

ACTIVITY CARD

TRANS CODE	SHORT PATH FLAG	SCHEDULE DATE	INTERFACE (B.E.)	BEGINNING EVENT NUMBER	LEVEL CODE (B.E.)	INTERFACE (E.E.)	ENDING EVENT NUMBER	LEVEL CODE (E.E.)	OPTIMISTIC TIME ACTIVITY FIELD NO 1	MOST LIKELY TIME ACTIVITY FIELD NO 2	PESSIMISTIC TIME ACTIVITY FIELD NO 3	SCHEDULED OR COMPLETED DATE			BLANK
												MO	DAY	YR ACTIVITY FIELD NO 4	
1	2	3	4 5	6 7 8 9 10 11 12 13	14	15 16 17	18 19 20 21 22 23	24	25 26 27 28	29 30 31 32	33 34 35 36	37 38	39 40	41 42	43

Column numbers (bottom): 1 2 3 4 5 6 7 8 9 10 11 12 13 14 15 16 17 18 19 20 21 22 23 24 25 26 27 28 29 30 31 32 33 34 35 36 37 38 39 40 41 42 43

AFSC FORM 30
JUL 63   PREVIOUS EDITIONS OF THIS FORM ARE OBSOLETE.

Figure 52.—U.S. Air Force PERT Time Input Form (Continued)

PAGE   OF   PAGES

Form Approved.
Budget Bureau Number 21—R208

OUTPUT HEADING

USER'S SYMBOL

BLANK

ACTIVITY OUTPUT

44	45	46	47	48	49	50	51	52	53	54	55	56	57	58	59	60	61	62	63	64	65	66	67	68	69	70	71	72	73	74	75	76	77	78	79	80

EVENT TITLE
(Ending Event)

BLANK   BLANK

ACTIVITY TITLE

BLANK   BLANK

44	45	46	47	48	49	50	51	52	53	54	55	56	57	58	59	60	61	62	63	64	65	66	67	68	69	70	71	72	73	74	75	76	77	78	79	80

44	45	46	47	48	49	50	51	52	53	54	55	56	57	58	59	60	61	62	63	64	65	66	67	68	69	70	71	72	73	74	75	76	77	78	79	80

75

allows the designation of milestone or master schedule events, a report can be generated listing only these particular items. Some programs also generate information regarding activity variance, event standard deviation, and probability statements. Such items usually appear on a line listing with the associated activity or event.

The options available in many computer programs present some problem in knowing which will be most useful. The most useful report is the Slack Path printout which shows the most Critical Path along with several limit paths in a network. Since primary project revision consists of shortening time on the Critical Path, this report should be reviewed first.

Most computer programs have built-in error messages; one of the most useful is the loop detector. This message indicates that someplace within a network is a circularity or a returning from a successor event back to an earlier predecessor event. In order to correct this error, the network must be inspected, using the "audit list" report, to find this loop. Other error messages may reveal that the network is not complete. In preparing the input deck, perhaps one activity was inadvertently omitted and hence one pathway is incomplete. Another useful error message consists of identifying incompatible dates. For example, possibly a completion date is assigned to an event whereas the preceding event has not yet been completed. Other error messages can be generated depending upon the particular computer program but the above are the most common types.

Careful attention must be paid to the preparation of data to be used in computer programs. A close check must be made against the network to be sure that event numbers are correct, that time estimates have been transferred correctly, and that all activities have been listed. Careful inspection before submission to the computer will prevent many errors and insure the accuracy of final data.

The cost of running or processing networks on the computer varies according to size of the network and the amount of information desired in the form of output reports, as well as on the particular computer used. If a relatively expensive computer is to be used, networks should be a sufficient size to justify the cost. Relatively small networks are perhaps best processed on a small computer. Another decision as to whether or not a computer program should be used rests upon the amount of staff effort involved in manual versus computer processing as well as the timeliness and accuracy of information desired. It is important to understand that one does not need a computer program with PERT, but once the networks become large, computer processing of data appears to be the only feasible expedient.

Reports

A generally recognized principle of management is that reports submitted to project directors and/or managers should be relatively simple and yet convey essential information. Project managers should not be forced to read voluminous data and detailed reports. The material should appear in such a form that problem areas can be identified quickly. Reports presented to managers should be either in a simple graphic or narrative form. Common types of reports presented to top level management under the PERT technique are the Project Outlook Report, the E–L or Milestone Report, and the PERT Analysis Report.

The Project Outlook Report usually shows the degree to which a project is running ahead, behind, or on schedule. Such a report is presented as figure 53.

The E–L chart usually lists selected milestone and/or master schedule events and plots on a time line, the Earliest Expected Date (E), and the Latest Allowable Date (L). A quick inspection of the chart reveals the amount of slack available between these two dates. An example of such an E–L chart is presented in figure 54.

The PERT Analysis Report consists of a narrative description of problems identified along with possible suggested solutions. Usually such a report is prepared by staff personnel within the project after careful analysis of data generated manually or by computers. An example of such a report is presented as figure 55. In this illustration, a problem is identified and possible impact noted, with alternative solutions and recommended actions. The manager is not committed to any of these alternatives but does have immediately available the thinking of persons working directly with the problem.

The frequency with which such reports are prepared and submitted to management vary from project to project. Some programs require biweekly reports while others require them only monthly. The value, however, lies in timeliness in reporting current conditions and in the information given with regard to problem areas and possible solutions. Delays in developing reports should be avoided since late information about problems prohibits the manager from applying corrective actions.

Project Updating

As the project moves along, the initial plan is invariably altered. New activities may be added, work completed behind or ahead of schedule, and the time estimates for on-going activities must be reestimated. The process of revising a project plan (or network) is referred to as "updating" and involves the actions listed or described below.

77

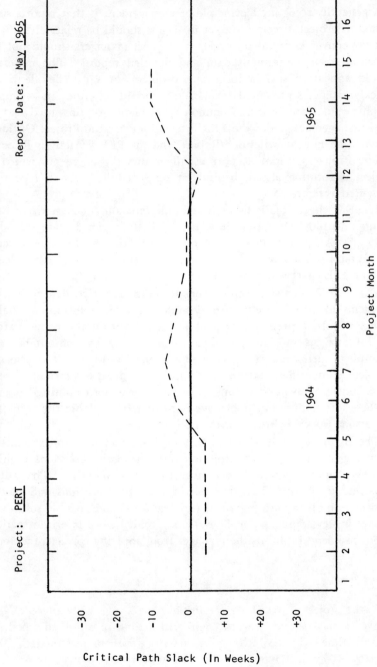

Figure 53.—Project Outlook Report Showing Project Slack Condition

Project: PERT

Report Date: May 1965

78

Figure 54.—Illustrative E-L Report for a Project

MASTER SCHEDULE OR MILESTONE REPORT

Project __G.E.D.__   Report Date __10-20-64__   Page __1__ of __1__ Pages

Event No.	Description	1964							1965						
		11-1	11-15	12-1	12-15	1-1	1-15	2-15	3-15	4-1	4-15	5-15	6-15	7-15	8-1
301	Review—Summarize Printout		E L												
307	Manuscript Acceptance							E L							
310	Monitor Completes Mailing									E L					
405	Project End													E L	

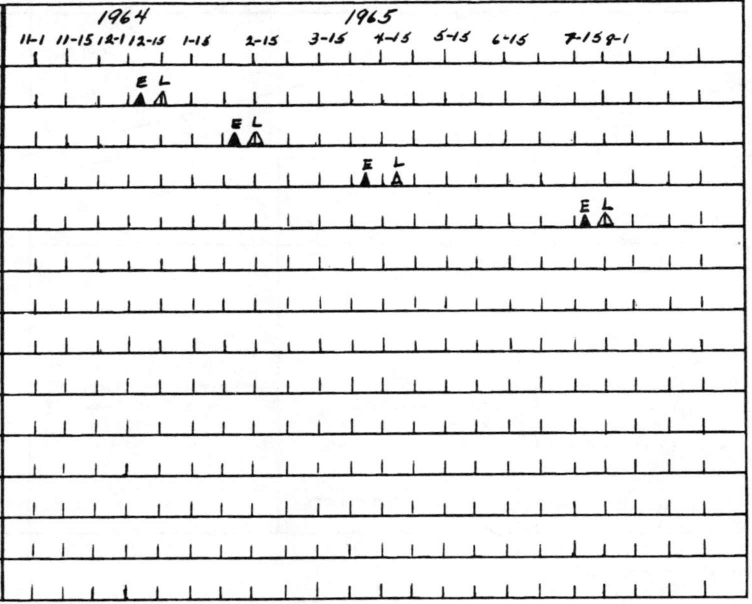

E = Earliest Expected Date   L = Latest Allowable Date

79

Figure 55.—PERT Analysis Report for Management Review

Project: PERT

Report Date: 5-21-65

PERT Analysis	Impact	Alternatives	Recommended Action	Management Decision
Problem: Total of 25.6 weeks required to submit final report according to present plan of which 12.7 weeks are required for art work planning and preparation.	Delay of final report submitted by 11 weeks	1. Request time extension 2. Re-evaluate art work requirements 3. Re-evaluate estimated time	1. Reduce art work 2. Simplify art work 3. Eliminate art work	Reduce and simplify art work
Problem:				
Problem:				

The most basic step in project updating is the securing of time estimates for new activities incorporated into the plan; estimates for time to completion for activities now in progress; and possible revision of time estimates for work yet to be accomplished which can now be more accurately defined. In the case of new activities, the process of securing time estimates from responsible management personnel is the same as in the original time estimating procedure. Activities currently in progress will have consumed some of the originally estimated time and will have further time to completion. A review of the work accomplished and yet to be done must be made in order to secure time estimates for completion of the activity. Notations made on the network as to the date of completion for an activity or the reaching of an event is a useful way of keeping track of activity completions. The project director or his associates should not trust to their memories as to the completion dates but rather should develop a system of recording dates as suggested. As progress is made during the project, quite possibly activities yet to be completed reflect time estimates based upon uncertainty associated with the nature of a task or an inability to define tasks far enough ahead to give valid time estimates. Revisions in activities not yet initiated can be made at this time, or they can remain as originally established until a succeeding update time.

Updating not only involves the reestimating of times as described above, but also includes certain mechanical procedures with regard to revising the graphical network. Major changes in the project plan should be incorporated into the network as soon as possible. Relatively minor changes in the project plan need not result in a modification of the network at the particular reporting period. Such changes can be accumulated over a defined period of time and then incorporated as a body. A practical way of keeping track of both types of change is to use a "Was-Is" chart, a copy of which appears as figure 56. Such a chart is useful in that it not only shows the project plan as it was and now is, but the necessary information with regard to changes in the data deck for computer runs can be transferred directly from the chart for keypunching purposes. Maintaining a file of such charts during the course of the project provides a useful way of studying the logic of the original plan once the project is completed. The project director should assign responsibility for incorporating necessary network changes to a member of his staff in order to insure that the desired changes are properly recorded. Since the network provides a useful visual tool for noting project status, changes should be recorded as soon as possible after reviews are made.

While a normal interval of project updating may occur, quite possibly some portions of the project which require management attention,

Figure 56.—Network Change (Was-Is) Worksheet

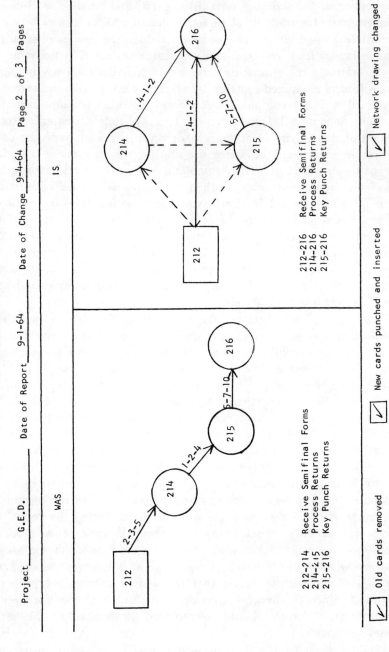

Project _____ G.E.D. _____   Date of Report _____ 9-1-64 _____   Date of Change _____ 9-4-64 _____

WAS

IS

212-214   Receive Semifinal Forms
214-215   Process Returns
215-216   Key Punch Returns

212-216   Receive Semifinal Forms
214-216   Process Returns
215-216   Key Punch Returns

Old cards removed   New cards punched and inserted   Network drawing changed

82

because of their importance or uniqueness, may be updated at more frequent intervals than the total project. Once such a portion of the total network has been completed, the frequency of reporting may be incorporated into a regular schedule.

Management Participation and Support

Fundamental to successful PERT applications is a firm decision to use PERT as the management planning and control tool for the entire project. Having made this decision, all participating project personnel should receive proper instruction in the technique. PERT will lose part, if not all, of its effectiveness as a management tool as well as become a burden to the project if it is used as a supplementary planning and control system without full project management support.

The project director should publish an early policy statement setting forth the role PERT will play in project management and control. The policy statement should be followed by assignment of responsibility to an organizational unit or a person for development of an implementation plan, for providing personnel training in the use of PERT, and for maintaining and updating the program plan during operational phases.

Implementation Checklist

The purpose of this chapter, as well as the monograph itself, is to present basic principles, procedures, and considerations involved in the implementation of PERT on a research and development program or project. The recommendations given should not be considered as absolute regulations or specific rules but rather as guidelines. In order to assist a new user who wants to insure that principal features of the system are considered, a PERT Implementation checklist is presented in figure 57.

The steps involved have been divided into two general topics: (1) Organizing for PERT Implementation, and (2) Operational Considerations. The first topic presents activities to be considered during preparation for use of PERT. The second topic presents, in general sequential order, the activities to be considered in an actual application from establishment of the work breakdown structure through to periodic updating of the project plan. In using this checklist, one should keep in mind that the degree of application can vary depending upon such factors as contractor requirements, internal management requirements, and project nature, duration, and complexity. PERT is a flexible management technique and should be adaptable as needed for adequate

Figure 57.—PERT Implementation Checklist

```
                    CHECKLIST FOR PERT IMPLEMENTATION

I. Organizing for PERT Implementation

    A.  Prepare policy statement on management support and participation.

    B.  Assignment of organizational responsibilities for PERT implementation
        and operation.

    C.  Secure PERT guidance documents.

    D.  Develop PERT implementation plan.

    E.  Prepare procedures handbook for PERT implementation to include such
        topics as:

        1.  Methods of preparing and transmitting input data during the
            original PERT application.

        2.  Methods for providing updating information as a result of
            computer processing or hand calculations.

        3.  Distribution system for output data and reports to persons
            having decision-making authority.

        4.  Types of management reports to be employed.

        5.  Establish frequency of reporting.

        6.  System for network preparation including event numbering, stan-
            dard activity descriptions, and designation of milestones.

        7.  Data input and output formats (depending on computer used) to
            be employed.

    F.  Conduct PERT training.
```

project planning and control.

Figure 57.—PERT Implementation Checklist (Continued)

II. Operational Considerations

    A. Work Breakdown Structure

        1. Develop work breakdown structure consistent with project proposal.

        2. Check to insure compatibility of work breakdown structure with proposal and contract items.

        3. Check end item subdivisions to insure coverage of all work contained in the summary item from which developed.

        4. Establish compatibility between work breakdown structure and the project organization.

        5. Assign organizational responsibility for work packages.

        6. Check to be sure work packages have well defined start and end points.

    B. Establish Network

        1. Develop master network to show general project plan.

        2. Develop detailed network and sub-networks based upon the master network and project work breakdown structure.

        3. Check events for uniqueness (i.e., occurring only once).

        4. Check network for possible "loops."

        5. Select project milestone events.

        6. Identify interface events.

        7. Check logic of final project network plan.

        8. Adopt event numbering system (sequential or random depending on computer program to be used).

        9. Secure time estimates for network activities.

Figure 57.—PERT Implementation Checklist (Continued)

C. Process Network Data

    1. Enter directed date on network.

    2. Transpose network event and activity data to keypunch input forms.

    3. Audit input forms against network for completeness and accuracy.

    4. Keypunch and verify PERT data.

    5. Process data.

D. Analysis and Replan

    1. Analyze computer output reports to note probability and slack conditions (i.e., problem areas).

    2. Verify reasonableness of problem by use of cross checks to locate errors in input data or processing.

    3. Analyze critical and limit paths to determine nature of constraints.

    4. Discuss possible problem areas with responsible organization or personnel for proposed solutions.

    5. Document proposed solutions of and prepare for reprocessing.

    6. Correct networks and reprocess data.

    7. Establish internal schedule dates, consistent directed schedule dates, and Latest Allowable Dates.

    8. Prepare reports and displays for management.

E. Update System

    1. Note completion dates for work elements accomplished.

    2. Secure time estimates for work elements in process.

    3. Review and secure as needed time estimates for work elements yet to be initiated.

    4. Incorporate management decisions into work breakdown structure and network.

    5. Process data.

Appendixes

Appendix I. Glossary of PERT Terms and Symbols

Terms

Activity

The work effort involving time and resources required to complete a task or job to a given level of performance. It is represented on the network by an arrow and connects two network events.

Activity Network

A network that uses activities rather than events as the basic building block.

Activity Slack

The difference in time between Earliest Completion Date (S_E) and Latest Completion Date (S_L) for a given activity. Activity slack indicates a space in time within which an activity may be scheduled for completion. If the S_E for an activity is later than the S_L, then the activity has negative slack and either the current activities or the subsequent activities must be replanned or the project schedule will fall behind. If the S_L for an activity is later than the S_E, then the activity has positive slack, and additional time is available for performing the activity without causing the project schedule to fall behind.

Activity Time Estimate

The estimate of the time necessary to complete an activity in a specific manner. This time is specified in weeks and/or tenths of weeks.

Activity Variance

A statistical statement of uncertainty based upon three time estimates for an activity using the following formula:

$$\sigma^2{}_{t_\bullet} = \left(\frac{b-a}{6}\right)^2$$

Constraint

The relationship of an event to a succeeding activity whereby the activity may not start until the preceding event has occurred. The term "constraint" is also used to indicate the relationship of an activity to a succeeding event whereby an event cannot occur until all preceding activities have been completed. Constraints can be planned or real.

Critical Path

That sequence of events and activities that has the greatest negative or least positive slack, or the longest path through the network. It is represented by a double-lined arrow.

Directed Date

The date of a specific accomplishment formally directed by the contract authority. It is usually represented by the symbol T_D.

Dummy Activity

A non-time-consuming activity used to illustrate event dependency. It is not descriptive of work and is represented on the network by a dashed-line arrow.

Earliest Completion Date

The earliest date on which a work effort (work package, activity, or summary item) can be completed. It is usually represented by the symbol S_E.

Earliest Expected Date

The earliest date on which an event may be expected to occur. It is usually represented by the symbol T_E. The Earliest Expected Date for a given event is equal to the sum of the Expected Elapsed Times (t_e) for the activities on the longest path from the beginning of the program to the given event.

End Item

A major project objective, usually a deliverable item of the contract.

Event

A specific, definable, accomplishment in a program network, which is recognizable at a particular instant in time. Events do not consume time or resources. They are usually represented on the network by circles.

Event Slack

The difference between the Earliest Expected Date (T_E) and the Latest Allowable Date (T_L) for a given event. If the T_E for an event is later than T_L, the event is said to have negative slack. When the T_L is later than the T_E, the event is said to have positive slack.

Expected Elapsed Time

The time which an activity is predicted to require based on the formula:

$$t_e = \frac{a + 4m + b}{6}$$

Expected Elasped Time is usually represented by the symbol t_e and has a 50-50 chance of being equalled or exceeded in practice.

Event Variance

The sum of activity variances $\left(\Sigma \sigma^2_{t_e} \right)$ on the longest path to an event.

Flow Chart

A pictorial description of a plan showing the interrelationships of all required events. It is also called a network, arrow diagram, etc.

Initial Event

An event which signifies the beginning of the network.

90

Interface

An interface defines the relationship that exists between various areas of any work effort. The interface ties together the events and activities within one area of work effort that constrains completion of events and activities in another area.

Interface Event

An event signalling a necessary transfer of responsibility, information, or end items from one part of a plan to another.

Latest Allowable Date

The latest date on which an event can occur without delaying completion of a program. It is usually represented by the symbol T_L.

Latest Completion Date

The latest calendar date on which a work effort (work package, activity, or summary item) can be scheduled for completion without delaying the completion of the program or project. It is represented by the symbol S_L.

Limit Path

Any path containing slack other than the Critical Path. The Critical Path is the most limiting path.

Milestones

Key program events the accomplishment of which are essential to the completion of a program. A milestone is usually represented on the network by a rectangle or square.

Most Likely Time

The most realistic estimate of the time an activity might consume in the opinion of the estimator. It is usually represented by the symbol (m). This time would be expected to occur more often than any other time if the activity could be repeated many times under the same circumstances.

Negative Slack

That amount of time in excess of the available time on a particular slack path predicted to be required to reach the objective event.

Network

A flow diagram consisting of activities and events which must be accomplished to reach the program objective. The flow diagram shows the planned sequences of accomplishment, interdependencies, and interrelationships of the activities and events.

Objective Event

The end or terminating event of the network.

Optimistic Time

The time in which an activity can be accomplished or completed if everything goes extremely well. It is represented by the symbol (a). An activity may have one chance in a hundred of being completed within this period.

Pessimistic Time

An estimate of the longest time an activity would require under the most adverse conditions. It is usually represented by the symbol (b). An activity may have one chance in a hundred of being completed within this period.

Positive Slack

The amount of extra time available to perform a series of activities in a particular path in support of the required completion date.

Predecessor Event

An event immediately preceding an activity arrow which signifies the completion of the previous activity and the start of a new activity.

Probability

A statistical statement of the likelihood of occurrence of a particular event in the network. It is represented by the symbol P_R.

Random Event Numbering

A system in which events are not numbered in any particular order.

Scheduled Completion Date

A date assigned for completion of an activity or event for purposes of planning and control. It is usually represented by the symbol T_S. Where no specific date is assigned, S_E equals T_S.

Sequential Event Numbering

A system in which each succeeding event has a number that is higher than the number of its preceding event.

Slack

The difference between the Latest Allowable Date and the Earliest Expected Date $(T_L - T_E)$. It is also the difference between the Latest Completion Date and the Earliest Completion Date $(S_L - S_E)$. Slack is a characteristic of the network paths. Slack may be positive, zero, or negative.

Slack Path

That path through a network along which all events have the same amount of slack.

Spread

An interval of time expressed in plus or minus weeks and tenths of weeks about the expected time (T_E) for an event which has a 50 percent probability statement.

Standard Deviation

A statistical statement of variability about the expected completion date of an activity. Common PERT practice uses a standard deviation equal to $\frac{1}{6}$ of the difference between the Optimistic and Pessimistic Time Estimates.

$$\sigma = \frac{b - a}{6}$$

Successor Event

An event signifying the termination point of one activity or the start of a new activity.

Task

A related group of activities that clearly defines a segment of a program. Small programs may be considered as one task while a system program may have a hundred or more. Tasks in a program are relatively stationary while activities are dynamic.

Time Estimate

An estimate of time required to perform an activity, based upon technical judgment, experience, and knowledge of the job. Time estimates are not commitments or schedules.

Time Now

Current calendar dates.

Work Breakdown Structure

A family tree subdivision of a project beginning with the end objective which is then subdivided into successively small units. The work breakdown structure establishes a framework for defining work to be accomplished, constructing a network plan, and summarizing the cost and schedule status of a project for progressively higher management levels.

Work Package

Work required to complete one or more specific activities. The content of the work package may be performed by a single working unit or by several working units. Overall responsibility for the work package is usually assigned to a single individual or department.

Symbols

a — The Optimistic Time Estimate for an activity when three time estimates are used.

b — The Pessimistic Time Estimate for an activity when three time estimates are used.

m — The Most Likely Time Estimate for an activity when three time estimates are used.

P_R — Probability for an event or activity being completed on time.

S_E — Earliest calendar completion date for an activity or event.

S_L — Latest calendar completion date for an activity or event.

T_D — A date for the completion of a specific event or activity, formally directed by the contracting authority.

t_e — The Expected Elapsed Time for an activity.

T_E — Earliest Expected Date for an event completion.

T_L — Latest Allowable Completion date for an event completion.

T_{O_E} — Earliest Expected Date for the objective or final event.

T_{O_S} — Scheduled date for the objective or final event.

t_s — The Scheduled Elapsed Time for an activity.

T_S — The Scheduled Completion Date for an activity or event assigned for purposes of internal project control.

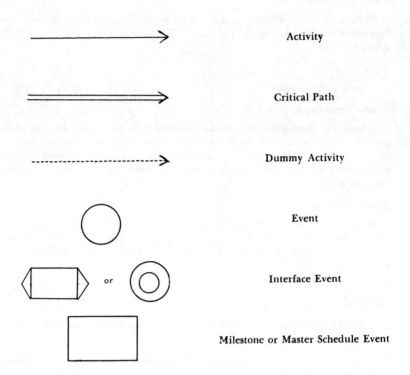

Activity

Critical Path

Dummy Activity

Event

Interface Event

Milestone or Master Schedule Event

Appendix II. Bibliography and Source Materials

References and Bibliography

Text References

1. ALBERTY, HAROLD J., and ALBERTY, ELSIE J. *Reorganizing the High School Curriculum,* 3d Ed. The MacMillan Co., New York, 1962.

2. AIR FORCE SYSTEMS COMMAND, ANDREWS AIR FORCE BASE. *USAF PERT—Vol. III, PERT COST System Description Manual.* Washington, D.C., December 1963.

3. AIR FORCE SYSTEMS COMMAND, ANDREWS AIR FORCE BASE. *USAF PERT—Vol. V, PERT Implementation Manual.* Washington, D.C., April 1964.

4. BACKSTROM, CHARLES H., and HURSH, GERALD D. *Survey Research.* Northwestern University Press, Evanston, Ill., 1963.

5. BENSON, ELLIS. *A Time and Sequence Analysis of Critical Steps in the Establishment of California Junior Colleges.* Unpublished doctoral dissertation, University of California at Los Angeles, 1963.

6. BORG, WALTER R. *Educational Research: An Introduction.* David McKay Co., Inc., New York, 1963.

7. CYPHERT, FREDERICK R. "Development of a Taxonomy for the Classification of Teacher Classroom Behavior." Cooperative Research Project No. 2288, May 22, 1963.

8. DEPARTMENT OF DEFENSE AND NATIONAL AERONAUTICS AND SPACE ADMINISTRATION GUIDE. *PERT Cost Systems Design.* Office of the Secretary of Defense, Washington, D.C., June 1962.

9. HUNGATE, T. L. *Management in Higher Education.* Bureau of Publications, Teachers College, Columbia University, New York, 1964.

10. KERLINGER, FRED N. *Foundations of Behavioral Research.* Holt, Rinehart, and Winston, Inc., New York, 1964.

11. LINDQUIST, E. F. (editor). *Educational Measurement.* American Council on Education, Washington, D.C., 1951.

12. LONGENECKER, JUSTIN G. *Principles of Management and Organizational Behavior.* Charles E. Merrill Books, Inc., Columbus, Ohio, 1964, Ch. 2.

13. MacCRIMMON, K. R., and RYAVEC, C. A. *An Analytical Study of the PERT Assumptions,* RM-3408-PR. The Rand Corporation Santa Monica, Calif., December 1962.

14. MALCOLM, D. G., ROSEBOOM, J. H., CLARK, C. E. and FAZAR, W. "Application of a Technique for Research and Development Program Evaluation." *Operations Research* 7:646-669, September-October 1959.

15. MILLER, DELBERT C. *Handbook of Research Design and Social Measurement.* David McKay Co., Inc., New York, 1964.

16. MILLER, ROBERT W. *Schedule, Cost, and Profit Control with PERT.* McGraw Hill Book Co., New York, 1963.

17. MOULY, GEORGE J. *The Science of Educational Research.* American Book Co., New York, 1963.

18. NATIONAL COUNCIL ON SCHOOLHOUSE CONSTRUCTION. *Guide for Planning School Plants.* Michigan State University, East Lansing, Mich., 1964.

19. PERT ORIENTATION AND TRAINING CENTER. *PERT Fundamentals.* Bolling Air Force Base, Washington, D.C., 1964.

20. PHILLIPS, C. R., and BEEK, CHARLES R. *Computer Programs for PERT and CPM.* 2d. ed. rev., Tech. Paper No. 13, Operations Research, Inc., Silver Spring, Md., October 1963.

21. SCHNEIDER, ERWIN H., and CADY, HENRY L. "Evaluation and Synthesis of Research Studies Relating to Music Education." Cooperative Research Project No. E-016, U. S. Office of Education, Sept. 24, 1963.

22. SMITH, EDWIN D. "The Use of PERT in Education," *The Proceedings of the Ninth College and University Machine Records Conference.* D. Morrison (ed). Monograph on Educational Data Processing No. 4, Educational Data Systems, 1964.

23. U. S. DEPARTMENT OF THE NAVY, SPECIAL PROJECTS OFFICE. *An Introduction to the PERT/COST System.* Washington, D.C., 1961

24. U. S. DEPARTMENT OF THE NAVY, BUREAU OF NAVAL WEAPONS, SPECIAL PROJECTS OFFICE. *PERT, Program Evaluation Research Task,* Summary Report, Phase I. Washington, D.C., July 1958.

25. U. S. DEPARTMENT OF THE NAVY, BUREAU OF NAVAL WEAPONS, SPECIAL PROJECTS OFFICE. *PERT, Program Evaluation Research Task,* Summary Report, Phase II. Washington, D.C., September 1958.

Selected Annotated Bibliography

1. AIR FORCE SYSTEMS COMMAND, USAF. *PERT and Other Network Techniques* (no date).

    An alphabetical listing of books, articles, presentations, and other papers relating to network techniques in general and PERT in particular.

2. ARMED SERVICES TECHNICAL INFORMATION AGENCY, DEFENSE DOCUMENTATION CENTER, (Elizabeth H. Hall, compiler). *PERT—A Report Bibliography.* March 13, 1963.

    A listing of 383 references covering ASTIA documents, books, journals, reports, conference proceedings, and monographs relating to PERT and PERT modifications. Covers the period October 1958, through February 1963.

3. BAKER, BRUCE N., and ERIS, RENE L. *An Introduction to PERT-CPM.* Richard D. Irwin, Inc., Homewood, Ill., 1964.

    Presents basic PERT procedures, an evaluation of PERT-CPM, some limitations and problems associated with PERT, along with a discussion of other network planning techniques.

4. BAUMAN, W. C. *PERT and Applied Research*. ASOOP Working Paper No. 3, Directorate of Technical Operations, Aeronautical Systems Division, Air Force Systems Command, Wright-Patterson Air Force Base, Dayton, Ohio, April 10, 1962.

Presents a discussion of the role PERT can play in applied research and development projects as opposed to basic research activities and production routine.

5. BAUMGARTNER, JOHN S. *Project Management*. Richard D. Irwin, Inc., Homewood, Ill., 1963.

A discussion of general problems and techniques of project management including such topics as the "project" concept, project planning, elements of control, and documentation. A basic description of PERT is presented as an appendix.

6. BOOZ, ALLEN, and HAMILTON (Management Consultants). *Management Implications of PERT*. New York, 1962.

A discussion of the way management can use the PERT technique prepared by the civilian consultant group involved in the original development of the PERT procedure.

7. BURNS, JOSEPH L. *A Catalog of Computer Programs for PERT*. Administrative Service Div., Westinghouse Electric Corp., Baltimore, Md. Dec. 15, 1963.

Presents a survey of PERT computer programs including program synopses, program descriptions, program characteristics, output reports, program modifications, and a list of users. Information was collected by Project SPERT (SHARE PERT) using a questionnaire.

8. COOK, DESMOND L. *An Introduction to PERT*. Occasional Paper 64-156, The Bureau of Educational Research and Service, The Ohio State University, Columbus, Ohio, 1964.

An elementary discussion of the principles of PERT with particular reference to its use in educational research and development projects.

9. DEAN, K. L. *Fundamentals of Network Planning and Analysis*. Military Dept., UNIVAC Div. of Sperry-Rand Corp., St. Paul, Minn., January 1962. (PX1842B).

A general outline of the principles of network planning underlying both PERT and CPM techniques for persons unfamiliar with network planning and analysis.

10. FAZAR, WILLARD, FOX, RONALD J., and LIVINGSTON, J. STERLING, "PERT Gains New Dimensions," *Aerospace Management* 5:32-36, January 1962.

An early and brief description of the initial application of the PERT/TIME concepts to the problem of determining activity costs. Selection of alternate time/cost options for purposes of meeting project deadlines is discussed. Concept of esource allocation" is presented.

11. KAHN, ARTHUR B. "Skeletal Structure of PERT and CPA Computer Programs," *Communications of the ACM* 6:473-479, August 1963.

Presents an introduction to the mechanics of PERT and Critical Path Analyses (CPA) Computer Programs. Outlines major components of such programs as well as their purposes and interrelationships.

12. LARSEN, R. P. "Program Evaluation and Review Technique Formulated for Digital Computer Application," Technical Information Series R60EML48, Light Military Electronics Division, General Electric Co., Utica, N.Y., June 15, 1960.

Formulates PERT's procedural mechanics using digital computer terminology assuming reader familiarity with PERT fundamentals. Emphasis is given to the analytical formulation of statistical time measures characterizing a scheduled program.

13. MURRAY, JOHN E. "Consideration of PERT Assumptions," *IEEE Transactions of the Professional Technical Group on Engineering Management*, V. EM 10, No. 3, September 1963.

Analysis of the original PERT statistical assumptions in view of experience gained with the technique. Cites reasons for establishment of original assumptions and suggests modifications designed to improve the statistical basis.

14. PERT COORDINATING GROUP, OFFICE OF THE SECRETARY OF DEFENSE. *PERT . . . Guide for Management Use*, Washington, D.C.

Description of PERT fundamentals so as to provide for a common means of communication between military, industrial, and governmental users.

15. PERT ORIENTATION AND TRAINING CENTER. *PERT and Other Management Systems and Techniques*. Bolling Air Force Base, Washington, D.C., June 1963.

An alphabetical compilation of books, magazine articles, technical documents covering PERT, and other management systems, for the period 1957 through June 1963. List consists of 702 references. Author index is provided.

16. RENINGER, NORMAND W. *A Study of the Network Concept of Planning Complex Projects*. Unpublished master's thesis, The Ohio State University, 1962.

A comparison of the characteristics of the network method of planning projects to the requirements of a good plan for the planning of projects as set forth by authorities in the area of business management.

17. RICE, ARTHUR H. "Let PERT Put You in the Driver's Seat," *Nation's Schools* 76:28-29, August 1965.

An editorial setting forth the values of PERT for school administrators.

18. STILIAN, GABRIEL, and others. *PERT: A New Management Planning and Control Technique*. American Management Association, New York, 1962.

A collection of 15 readings dealing with the relationship between management and PERT, PERT theory, practical experiences with PERT, and PERT variations.

19. STIRES, D. M. and MURPHY, M. M. *Modern Management Methods—PERT and CPM*. Materials Management Institute, Boston, Mass., 1962.

Discusses in elementary fashion the fundamentals of and the differences between two highly similar management planning and control tools. Sample problems are presented along with a glossary of terms.

20. STIRES, DAVID M., and WENIG, RAYMOND P. *PERT/COST—Concepts, Principles, Applications*. Industrial Education Institute, Boston, Mass., 1964.

A text designed to develop a working knowledge of information and procedures for PERT/COST implementation, using the case problem method. Conforms to DOD and NASA PERT/COST guidelines.

21. THIER, HERBERT D. *PERT and the Administration of Curriculum Innovation.* Science Curriculum Improvement Study, University of California, Berkeley. (mimeo).

A discussion of the possible role PERT can play in planning the development of a new curriculum in science for grades K-6.

22. U. S. DEPARTMENT OF THE NAVY, SPECIAL PROJECTS OFFICE. "Common Problems Associated with Implementation and Operations of the PERT/COST System," PERT Coordinating Group Technical Paper No. 1, Washington, D.C., 20360.

Discusses basic features of the PERT/COST system and presents common implementation problems with accompanying symptoms and recommended actions.